1st Workshop on Transcript Understanding (TU 2022)

Gyeongju, South Korea
12-17 October 2022

ISBN: 978-1-7138-6198-0

Printed from e-media with permission by:

Curran Associates, Inc.
57 Morehouse Lane
Red Hook, NY 12571

CURRAN ASSOCIATES INC. proceedings.com

Some format issues inherent in the e-media version may also appear in this print version.

Printed with permission by Curran Associates, Inc. (2023)

Association for Computational Linguistics
209 N. Eighth Street
Stroudsburg, Pennsylvania 18360

Phone: 1-570-476-8006
Fax: 1-570-476-0860

acl@aclweb.org

Additional copies of this publication are available from:

Curran Associates, Inc.
57 Morehouse Lane
Red Hook, NY 12571 USA
Phone: 845-758-0400
Fax: 845-758-2633
Email: curran@proceedings.com
Web: www.proceedings.com

COLING

International Conference on Computational Linguistics

Proceedings of the Conference and Workshops

COLING

Volume 29 (2022), No. 11

Proceedings of 1st Workshop on Transcript Understanding (TU)

The 29th International Conference on Computational Linguistics

October 12 - 17, 2022
Gyeongju, Republic of Korea

Message from the General Chair and the Program Chairs

Welcome to the 1st Workshop on Transcript Understanding (TU 2022)!

We are pleased to present the accepted papers at TU 2022. The workshop was held as a hybrid conference following COLING 2022 on October 16th-17th, 2022.

TU 2022 accepts papers through the START system. The submitted papers were double-blind reviewed by our program committee. In total, five papers were accepted. Their topics include:

- Dialogue summarization
- Dialogue understanding and generation
- Event tracking
- Machine translation
- Discourse relation recognition

We are also very excited to have an excellent speaker, **Dr. Fei Liu**, associate professor from department of Computer Science at the University of Central Florida, discussing recent advances and challenges in natural language processing and deep learning.

We are deeply thankful to all reviewers for their invaluable evaluation of the program selection and the authors' feedback. We thank all program chairs and publication chairs for their effort in compiling the workshop.

Franck Dernoncourt, General Chair

Viet Dac Lai, Program Co-Chair

People

General Chair

Franck Dernoncourt, Thien Huu Nguyen.

Program Chair

Viet Dac Lai, Amir Pouran Ben Veyseh, Trung H. Bui, David Seunghyun Yoon.

Program Committee

Amir Pouran Ben Veyseh, Minh Van Nguyen, Nghia Trung Ngo, Abel Salinas, Long Phan, Son Tran.

Table of Contents

Conference Program

Leveraging Non-dialogue Summaries for Dialogue Summarization
Seongmin Park, Dongchan Shin and Jihwa Lee

Knowledge Transfer with Visual Prompt in multi-modal Dialogue Understanding and Generation
minjun zhu, Yixuan Weng, Bin Li, Shizhu He, Kang Liu and Jun Zhao

Model Transfer for Event tracking as Transcript Understanding for Videos of Small Group Interaction
Sumit Agarwal, Rosanna Vitiello and Carolyn Rosé

BehanceMT: A Machine Translation Corpus for Livestreaming Video Transcripts
Minh Van Nguyen, Franck Dernoncourt and Thien Nguyen

Investigating the Impact of ASR Errors on Spoken Implicit Discourse Relation Recognition
Linh The Nguyen and Dat Quoc Nguyen

Leveraging Non-dialogue Summaries for Dialogue Summarization

Seongmin Park **Dongchan Shin** **Jihwa Lee**
ActionPower
Seoul, Republic of Korea
{seongmin.park, dongchan.shin, jihwa.lee}@actionpower.kr

Abstract

To mitigate the lack of diverse dialogue summarization datasets in academia, we present methods to utilize non-dialogue summarization data for enhancing dialogue summarization systems. We apply transformations to document summarization data pairs to create training data that better befit dialogue summarization. The suggested transformations also retain desirable properties of non-dialogue datasets, such as improved faithfulness to the source text. We conduct extensive experiments across both English and Korean to verify our approach. Although absolute gains in ROUGE naturally plateau as more dialogue summarization samples are introduced, utilizing non-dialogue data for training significantly improves summarization performance in zero- and few-shot settings and enhances faithfulness across all training regimes.

1 Introduction

Dialogue summarization fundamentally differs from its non-dialogue counterparts in two ways: the presence of speaker information and the inherent abstractiveness that demands any dialogue summarization system to "read between the lines". Consequently, training a dialogue summarization model requires datasets appropriate for the dialogue domain, which often calls for different provisions than those commonly found in traditional, non-dialogue summarization datasets.

The bulk of research efforts in summarization, however, has historically been focused on written documents. As a result, the research community faces a shortage of diverse dialogue summarization data, in contrast to the abundance of non-dialogue summarization data (Feng et al., 2021; Tuggener et al., 2021). From such state of the literature, we identify a strong need for methods to utilize widely available non-dialogue summarization data in reinforcing dialogue summarization models.

In this work, we present recipes to transform non-dialogue data into formats that enable direct integration into dialogue summarization training. During the transformation process, we also inherit desirable properties that arise from the extractiveness of non-dialogue summarization datasets. Factual inconsistency and hallucination are major research problems in dialogue summarization (Maynez et al., 2020; Ladhak et al., 2021; Cao et al., 2018; Huang et al., 2021). Since extractive summaries naturally remain more faithful to the source text, we design our transformation schemes to retain such properties when adapting non-dialogue summary data to the dialogue domain.

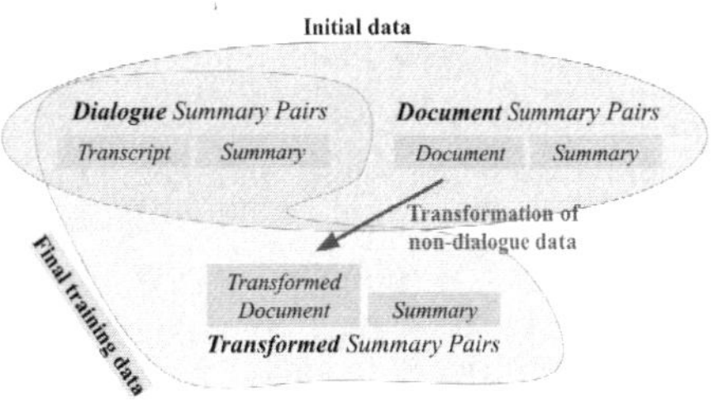

Figure 1: Overview of our proposed method. We transform non-dialogue data into a format exploitable by dialogue summarization models.

Our contributions are as follows:

1. We present formulas to transform non-dialogue summarization datasets into patterns usable for dialogue summarization. Summarization models trained with the additional data produce summaries more similar to gold reference summaries.

2. We show that utilizing non-dialogue summarization data preserves faithfulness in otherwise factually-unchecked summaries.

3. We test our data manipulation scheme across two languages (English and Korean) and on document summary datasets with different levels of abstraction.

Proceedings of the 29th International Conference on Computational Linguistic, pages 1–7
October 12–17, 2022.

In Section 2, we first describe existing challenges in dialogue summarization. In Section 3, we describe our dataset adaptation methods in detail. In Section 4, we describe datasets, evaluation metrics, and experiments used to test our methods.

2 Related works

2.1 Non-dialogue data for dialogue summarization

Even in high-resource languages like English, diversely annotated dialogue summarization datasets are scarce (Feng et al., 2021; Tuggener et al., 2021; Zou et al., 2021). The need for a diverse collection of dialogue summarization datasets is further exacerbated by the fact that dialogue is recorded in many formats, such as meetings, chats, and spontaneous speech.

To appease such a need for more data, several attempts have been made to utilize non-dialogue data in dialogue summarization (Figure 1). (Zou et al., 2021) pre-trains a language model with BookCorpus (Zhu et al., 2015) to provide training samples across diverse domains. (Khalifa et al., 2021) pre-trains BART (Lewis et al., 2020) with unlabeled dialogue corpora and fine-tunes the language model with downstream summary tasks.

The focus of such approaches lies in whetting a model to be more responsive to limited dialogue summarization data. We suggest a new line of research that directly manipulates the training data instead of steering a model's disposition directly.

2.2 Faithfulness in dialogue summarization

Factual incorrectness is a problem commonly observed in abstractive summarization systems (Cao et al., 2018; Huang et al., 2021; Tang et al., 2021). Tang et al. (2021) identifies categories of factual errors that dialogue summarization models may generate. To improve the factual consistencies of generated summaries, the authors corrupt dialogue transcripts to create negative samples in a contrastive-learning scheme.

We employ a similar noising approach. Negative sample generation in (Tang et al., 2021) requires accurate token-level operations, such as part-of-speech extraction and word negation. Our manipulation scheme forgoes such additional components, relying only on deterministic sentence-level edits.

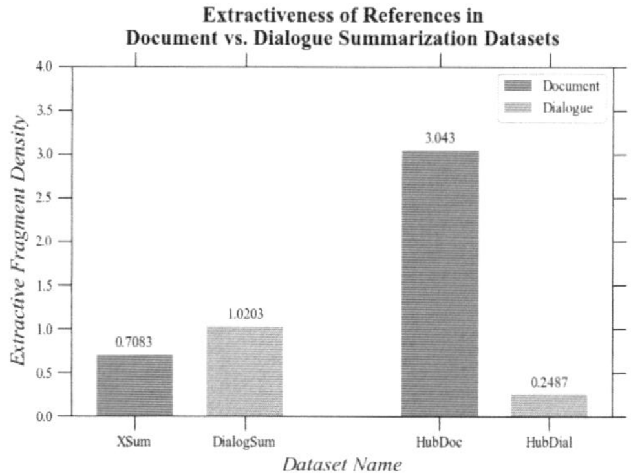

Figure 2: Extractiveness of reference summaries. Extractive Fragment Density (Grusky et al., 2018) is the longest extractive token span from the source data that matches the reference summary.

3 Proposed method

3.1 Preliminaries

Let

$$DocSet = \{(A_0, X_0), (A_1, X_1), ..., (A_i, X_i)\} \quad (1)$$

be a non-dialogue (document) summarization dataset, where A_i is the i-th document in the set, and X_i is the corresponding reference summary. A_i is a sequence of sentences $(a_0, a_1, ..., a_m)$, where m is the sentence count.

Similarly, we define a dialogue summarization dataset,

$$DialSet = \{(B_0, Y_0), (B_1, Y_1), ..., (B_j, Y_j)\}, \quad (2)$$

where B_j is the j-th dialogue transcript in the dataset, and Y_j is the corresponding dialogue summary. Like any A, B_j consists of ordered sentences $(b_0, b_1, ..., b_n)$.

We define $F = \{f_0, ..., f_k\}$, a set of *transformation functions* to be applied to each A_i in $DocSet$. A transformation function is a set of operations to transform non-dialogue text data into a pattern usable in dialogue summarization training.

We introduce three such transformation functions: **forcing plain text into dialogue format** (e.g. by inserting pseudo-speaker information), **shuffling sentence order**, and **omitting the sentence with highest extractive overlap** with the reference summary. Each suggested transformation function is formerly defined in succeeding sections.

Once f_k is applied to each A_i in $DocSet$, each transformed non-dialogue input text is paired with

Table 1: Evaluation metrics for full training. f_d (D) transformation is consistently effective in boosting match-based ROUGE. Even though marginal gain in ROUGE from our method naturally decreases as the size of $DialSet$ increases, incorporating document summarization data greatly improves summary faithfulness. R1, R2, RL, Prec., Rec., Faith. respectively stands for ROUGE-1, ROUGE-2, ROUGE-L, Precision, Recall, and Faithfulness. Underlined values are the highest in each column. Higher is better for all metrics.

Data	DialogSum						HubDial					
	R1	*R2*	*RL*	*Prec.*	*Rec.*	*Faith.*	*R1*	*R2*	*RL*	*Prec.*	*Rec.*	*Faith.*
Original	39.57	15.43	32.97	-3.8962	-4.3175	-4.1101	35.42	16.90	31.11	-9.9774	-9.7934	-8.9965
Naive	39.36	14.89	32.56	-2.9108	-2.9933	-2.5351	35.97	17.68	31.13	-7.8063	-7.6203	-7.9189
D	**40.47**	**16.41**	**33.89**	**-2.9085**	-2.8702	-2.4615	**36.32**	17.61	**31.79**	**-7.7715**	-7.6190	-7.9202
S	39.94	15.70	33.31	-2.9310	-2.8966	-2.4261	36.08	**18.13**	31.41	-7.8159	**-7.5791**	**-7.8610**
O	39.80	15.97	33.32	-2.9211	**-2.8253**	**-2.4072**	35.96	17.51	31.32	-7.7975	-7.6251	-7.8954
D + S	39.87	15.73	33.44	-2.9235	-2.9224	-2.4970	36.03	**17.55**	**31.93**	-7.8179	-7.6066	**-7.9104**
D + O	**40.66**	**16.77**	**34.15**	**-2.9044**	**-2.8073**	**-2.4196**	36.11	17.52	31.92	**-7.7776**	-7.6245	-7.9395
S + O	40.34	16.33	33.82	-2.9077	-2.8797	-2.4376	35.52	17.21	31.32	-7.8456	-7.6149	-7.9244
D + S + O	39.97	16.00	33.56	-2.9402	-2.8678	-2.4278	**36.26**	17.29	31.29	-7.8105	**-7.5956**	-7.9371

its corresponding reference X_i to form a new training set:

$$NewDocSet = \{(f_k(A), X) \mid (A, X) \in DocSet\}. \tag{3}$$

$NewDocSet$ can be used as additional training data for dialogue summarization models.

3.2 Arranging text into dialogue format (f_d)

Given a plain document, we convert its contents into transcript format by segmenting the document into sentences and appending a psuedo speaker:

$$f_d(A) = (concatenate(\text{"}Speaker\ 1:\text{"},\ a))_{a \in A}. \tag{4}$$

This operation serves two purposes: we prime our model to be more receptive of dialogue-formatted data through prompting (Liu et al., 2021). We also remove the gap between data patterns in training and inference by standardizing diverse non-dialogue document data into the dialogue domain.

The prompt *"Speaker 1"* was chosen empirically: multiple configurations, such as varying speaker numbers and inserting real names, were tested. Such complex configurations led to only marginal increases in evaluation metrics and introduced additional roadblocks in reliable reproduction (upper bound in speaker number has to be arbitrarily selected; a dictionary with realistic names has to be distributed). Both English and Korean datasets used *"Speaker 1"*.

3.3 Shuffling sentence order (f_d)

To combat lead bias commonly observed in traditional summarization datasets (Grenander et al., 2019; Zhu et al., 2021), we shuffle the order of sentences in A:

$$f_s(A) = shuffle(A). \tag{5}$$

Previous research has shown sentence shuffling helps in reducing read bias (Grenander et al., 2019). Since information in dialogues is often dispersed across multiple utterances, we find sentence shuffling to be more impactful when dealing with dialogues, compared to documents.

3.4 Omitting the most extractive sentence (f_o)

Among all sentences in a document, we delete the sentence with the most extractive overlap with the reference summary. The degree of overlap is calculated by the number of shared character 3-grams between a single sentence from the source document and the whole reference.

$$f_o(A_i) = A_i\{a_{ex}\}, \tag{6}$$

where a_{ex} in A_i has the highest 3-gram overlap with X_i. By removing the most extractive sentence, we aim to make $DocSet$ more abstractive and reduce copying behavior.

Table 2: Datasets used in the experiment. "Dial." and "Doc." stand for "dialogue" and "document".

Name	**Lang.**	**Type**	**Size**	**Abstractive?**
DialogSum	English	Dial.	15,600	Yes
XSum	English	Doc.	204,045	Yes
HubDial	Korean	Dial.	16,000	Yes
HubDoc	Korean	Doc.	334,160	No

4 Experiments

4.1 Experiment setup

We conduct comprehensive experiments that apply transformation functions defined in Section 3.

4.1.1 Our models

First, we create different variants of $NewDocSet$ by applying functions in $F = \{f_d, f_s, f_o\}$ both individually and in combination. Such application results in 7 different variations of $NewDocSet$: D, O, S, $D+O$, $D+S$, $S+O$, $D+S+O$, where, for example, $D+O = \{f_d \circ f_o(A) \mid A \in DocSet\}$.

With newly acquired training data, we train a BART-base (Lewis et al., 2020; Wolf et al., 2019) summarizer under three different configurations:

1. *Zero-shot*: $NewDocSet$ is the training set.

2. *Few-shot*: Training data consists of $NewDocSet$ and 100 or 1000 samples from $DialSet$.

3. *Full training*: Training data consists of $NewDocSet + DialSet$.

We choose the BART architecture due to its widespread use and proven track record in summarization (Fabbri et al., 2021; Akiyama et al., 2021; Zhao et al., 2021).

4.1.2 Baselines

We compare our trained models with two baselines:

1. *Original*: $DialSet$ is the training set.

2. *Naive*: Training data consists of $DialSet$ and $DocSet$ (i.e. $f_{naive}(A) = A$).

4.2 Datasets

For English, we use DialogSum (Chen et al., 2021) as $DialSet$ and XSum (Narayan et al., 2018) as $DocSet$. For Korean, we use AIHub Dialogue Summarization Dataset[1] (HubDial) as $DialSet$ and AIHub Document Summarization Dataset[2] (HubDoc) as $DocSet$. Table 2 contains a brief description of each dataset.

Transformations f_s and f_o hinge on the assumption that non-dialogue summarization datasets typically display considerable lead bias and are more extractive than dialogue summarization datasets. To gauge how extractiveness of non-dialogue data effects final summary generation performance, we conduct experiments on both highly extractive (HubDoc) and extremely abstractive (XSum) document summarization datasets (Figure 2).

4.3 Evaluation metrics

Performance of our model is measured as the similarity between model summaries and reference summaries, calculated with standard ROUGE scores (ROUGE-1, ROUGE-2, and ROUGE-L) (Lin, 2004). We also measure the faithfulness of the output summaries to input dialogues with BartScore (Yuan et al., 2021). BartScore is a state-of-the-art evaluation metric for factual consistency and faithfulness in text generation.

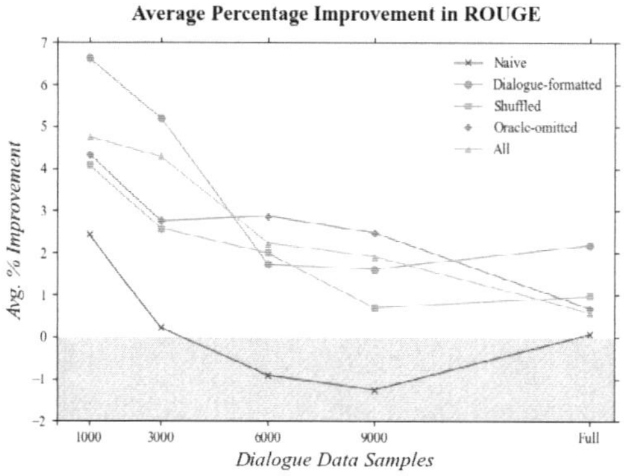

Figure 3: Averaged percentage ROUGE-1, ROUGE-2, and ROUGE-L improvements over dialogue-only training on HubDial test set. Shaded regions indicate configurations that underperform dialogue-only training.

5 Results

5.1 Full training

Both English and Korean summarization models benefit from additional data curated by our transformation functions. Only naive application of non-dialogue data fails to improve ROUGE scores compared to dialogue-only training. While marginal increase in ROUGE saturates as more dialogue summaization training samples are added, the addition of document data significantly enhances factual consistency of summaries (Table 1).

5.1.1 Abstractive document summary dataset

In terms of ROUGE, models trained with abstractive document summarization data (XSum) are most affected by f_d (D) transformations. Highest scoring data transformation combinations mostly

[1] https://aihub.or.kr/aidata/30714
[2] https://aihub.or.kr/aidata/8054

Table 3: Few-shot results on English DialogSum. Since XSum is already highly abstractive, f_d (D) transformation is the most effective. Almost all maximum values in each category involve a f_d transformation. Notations are the same as in Table 1.

	Zero-shot				100-shot				1000-shot			
	R1	*R2*	*RL*	*Faith.*	*R1*	*R2*	*RL*	*Faith.*	*R1*	*R2*	*RL*	*Faith.*
Original	-	-	-	-	31.05	10.55	26.58	-4.4925	35.12	12.23	29.20	-4.7314
Naive	13.64	2.71	11.21	-2.9081	31.05	9.31	25.81	-4.5829	37.97	13.22	31.11	-2.4799
D	15.46	3.18	13.05	**-2.7045**	**34.93**	**10.74**	**28.21**	-4.4414	38.28	13.23	31.08	-2.4319
S	14.35	**3.51**	12.11	-2.8926	32.83	09.82	26.80	**-2.4675**	**38.33**	13.62	**31.45**	**-2.4146**
O	**16.41**	2.80	**13.66**	-2.9846	32.89	09.53	27.24	-2.8102	38.28	**13.57**	31.12	-2.4495
D + S	**17.47**	**4.27**	**14.56**	**-2.4899**	34.51	**10.96**	27.96	-2.7527	38.26	13.27	31.21	-2.4494
D + O	14.73	2.88	12.07	-2.9530	34.40	10.76	28.18	**-2.6696**	**38.85**	**13.55**	**31.62**	**-2.3949**
S + O	16.69	3.42	13.96	-3.1872	33.84	10.27	27.83	-3.0668	38.55	13.44	31.19	-2.4154
D + S + O	16.36	3.84	13.76	-2.5456	**34.65**	10.82	**28.25**	-2.7152	36.80	13.03	30.42	-2.4381

Table 4: Few-shot results on Korean HubDial. Compared to less extractive English summarization, we see f_s (S) and f_o (O) transformations resulting in greater marginal increase in ROUGE. Notations are the same as in Table 1.

	Zero-shot				100-shot				1000-shot			
	R1	*R2*	*RL*	*Faith.*	*R1*	*R2*	*RL*	*Faith.*	*R1*	*R2*	*RL*	*Faith.*
Original	-	-	-	-	3.41	1.35	3.03	-10.2144	31.42	13.64	26.69	-7.9586
Naive	20.72	8.94	18.34	-7.4637	27.98	12.56	24.24	-7.7524	32.17	14.74	27.34	-7.8893
D	**26.34**	**11.74**	**22.97**	-7.6731	28.48	13.03	24.79	**-7.6451**	**33.05**	**15.16**	**28.46**	**-7.7255**
S	21.38	9.43	19.01	-7.3379	28.12	12.42	24.19	-7.9053	32.68	14.91	27.78	-7.8162
O	22.09	9.82	19.73	**-7.1363**	**29.50**	**13.26**	**25.01**	-7.8737	32.26	14.77	27.85	-7.8357
D + S	24.21	11.31	21.48	-7.8747	28.50	13.06	24.84	-7.8565	31.78	14.62	27.18	-7.7687
D + O	**24.81**	11.20	**22.04**	-7.7556	29.71	13.17	**25.68**	**-7.8058**	31.67	14.66	27.33	**-7.7651**
S + O	20.38	9.25	18.50	**-7.4731**	**29.79**	**13.47**	25.62	-7.9142	31.92	14.53	27.16	-7.7673
D + S + O	24.17	**11.37**	21.46	-7.8234	28.50	13.31	24.48	-7.8908	**32.77**	15.25	**27.96**	-7.7934

involve f_d. In terms of factual consistency and faithfulness, f_o transformations consistently score the highest. This is in line with our intention to introduce an additional in-comprehension understanding objective to the model that simple dialogue formatting cannot provide.

5.1.2 Extractive document summary dataset

f_s (S) and f_o (O) transformations are more influential when used to transform extractive data (HubDoc). Factual consistency is correlated the most with f_s, because of lead bias present in HubDoc.

5.2 Zero- and few-shot training

In zero- and full-shot training, we see significant improvements in both ROUGE and factual consistency (Tables 3, 4). Figure 3 shows improvements in ROUGE over $DialSet$-only training at different dialogue $DialSet$ sizes. Naively training with non-dialogue summarization data yields results no better than training with only dialogue data. In contrast, our suggested transformations provide significant gains in both span match and consistency measures in low-shot training regimes.

Comparative influence of each transformation function (f_d, f_s, and f_o) show trends similar to those observed in full training, with f_d proving the most dominant for already abstractive $DocSet$ (XSum) and f_s and f_o being more influential in comparatively extractive $DocSet$ (HubDoc).

6 Conclusion

We present simple but immediately effective methods to utilize abundant non-dialogue summarization data to improve dialogue summarization systems. We evaluate performance gains in similarity to reference summaries as well as in factual consistency to original transcript input. We find that our method is especially impactful in low-resource dialogue summarization.

Our research hints at two possible avenues for further investigation: reinforcing the three presented transformation recipes with a more methodical generation of prompts (Ghazvininejad et al., 2021), or introducing new transformations that better capture the unique properties of dialogue summarization datasets.

References

Kazuki Akiyama, Akihiro Tamura, and Takashi Ninomiya. 2021. Hie-BART: Document summarization with hierarchical BART. In *Proceedings of the 2021 Conference of the North American Chapter of the Association for Computational Linguistics: Student Research Workshop*, pages 159–165, Online. Association for Computational Linguistics.

Ziqiang Cao, Furu Wei, Wenjie Li, and Sujian Li. 2018. Faithful to the original: Fact aware neural abstractive summarization. In *thirty-second AAAI conference on artificial intelligence*.

Yulong Chen, Yang Liu, Liang Chen, and Yue Zhang. 2021. DialogSum: A real-life scenario dialogue summarization dataset. In *Findings of the Association for Computational Linguistics: ACL-IJCNLP 2021*, pages 5062–5074, Online. Association for Computational Linguistics.

Alexander R. Fabbri, Faiaz Rahman, Imad Rizvi, Borui Wang, Haoran Li, Yashar Mehdad, and Dragomir Radev. 2021. Convosumm: Conversation summarization benchmark and improved abstractive summarization with argument mining. In *ACL-IJCNLP 2021*.

Xiachong Feng, Xiaocheng Feng, and Bing Qin. 2021. A survey on dialogue summarization: Recent advances and new frontiers. *arXiv preprint arXiv:2107.03175*.

Marjan Ghazvininejad, Vladimir Karpukhin, and Asli Celikyilmaz. 2021. Discourse-aware prompt design for text generation. *CoRR*, abs/2112.05717.

Matt Grenander, Yue Dong, Jackie Chi Kit Cheung, and Annie Louis. 2019. Countering the effects of lead bias in news summarization via multi-stage training and auxiliary losses. In *Proceedings of the 2019 Conference on Empirical Methods in Natural Language Processing and the 9th International Joint Conference on Natural Language Processing (EMNLP-IJCNLP)*, pages 6019–6024, Hong Kong, China. Association for Computational Linguistics.

Max Grusky, Mor Naaman, and Yoav Artzi. 2018. Newsroom: A dataset of 1.3 million summaries with diverse extractive strategies. In *Proceedings of the 2018 Conference of the North American Chapter of the Association for Computational Linguistics: Human Language Technologies, Volume 1 (Long Papers)*, pages 708–719, New Orleans, Louisiana. Association for Computational Linguistics.

Yichong Huang, Xiachong Feng, Xiaocheng Feng, and Bing Qin. 2021. The factual inconsistency problem in abstractive text summarization: A survey. *arXiv preprint arXiv:2104.14839*.

Muhammad Khalifa, Miguel Ballesteros, and Kathleen McKeown. 2021. A bag of tricks for dialogue summarization. In *Proceedings of the 2021 Conference on Empirical Methods in Natural Language Processing*, pages 8014–8022, Online and Punta Cana, Dominican Republic. Association for Computational Linguistics.

Faisal Ladhak, Esin Durmus, He He, Claire Cardie, and Kathleen McKeown. 2021. Faithful or extractive? on mitigating the faithfulness-abstractiveness trade-off in abstractive summarization. *arXiv preprint arXiv:2108.13684*.

Mike Lewis, Yinhan Liu, Naman Goyal, Marjan Ghazvininejad, Abdelrahman Mohamed, Omer Levy, Veselin Stoyanov, and Luke Zettlemoyer. 2020. BART: Denoising sequence-to-sequence pre-training for natural language generation, translation, and comprehension. In *Proceedings of the 58th Annual Meeting of the Association for Computational Linguistics*, pages 7871–7880, Online. Association for Computational Linguistics.

Chin-Yew Lin. 2004. ROUGE: A package for automatic evaluation of summaries. In *Text Summarization Branches Out*, pages 74–81, Barcelona, Spain. Association for Computational Linguistics.

Pengfei Liu, Weizhe Yuan, Jinlan Fu, Zhengbao Jiang, Hiroaki Hayashi, and Graham Neubig. 2021. Pre-train, prompt, and predict: A systematic survey of prompting methods in natural language processing. *arXiv preprint arXiv:2107.13586*.

Joshua Maynez, Shashi Narayan, Bernd Bohnet, and Ryan McDonald. 2020. On faithfulness and factuality in abstractive summarization. In *Proceedings of the 58th Annual Meeting of the Association for Computational Linguistics*, pages 1906–1919, Online. Association for Computational Linguistics.

Shashi Narayan, Shay B. Cohen, and Mirella Lapata. 2018. Don't give me the details, just the summary! Topic-aware convolutional neural networks for extreme summarization. In *Proceedings of the 2018 Conference on Empirical Methods in Natural Language Processing*, Brussels, Belgium.

Xiangru Tang, Arjun Nair, Borui Wang, Bingyao Wang, Jai Desai, Aaron Wade, Haoran Li, Asli Celikyilmaz, Yashar Mehdad, and Dragomir Radev. 2021. Confit: Toward faithful dialogue summarization with linguistically-informed contrastive fine-tuning. *arXiv preprint arXiv:2112.08713*.

Don Tuggener, Margot Mieskes, Jan Deriu, and Mark Cieliebak. 2021. Are we summarizing the right way? a survey of dialogue summarization data sets. In *Proceedings of the Third Workshop on New Frontiers in Summarization*, pages 107–118, Online and in Dominican Republic. Association for Computational Linguistics.

Thomas Wolf, Lysandre Debut, Victor Sanh, Julien Chaumond, Clement Delangue, Anthony Moi, Pierric Cistac, Tim Rault, Rémi Louf, Morgan Funtowicz, et al. 2019. Huggingface's transformers: State-of-the-art natural language processing. *arXiv preprint arXiv:1910.03771*.

Weizhe Yuan, Graham Neubig, and Pengfei Liu. 2021. Bartscore: Evaluating generated text as text generation. *Advances in Neural Information Processing Systems*, 34.

Lulu Zhao, Fujia Zheng, Keqing He, Weihao Zeng, Yuejie Lei, Huixing Jiang, Wei Wu, Weiran Xu, Jun Guo, and Fanyu Meng. 2021. Todsum: Task-oriented dialogue summarization with state tracking. *arXiv preprint arXiv:2110.12680*.

Chenguang Zhu, Ziyi Yang, Robert Gmyr, Michael Zeng, and Xuedong Huang. 2021. Leveraging lead bias for zero-shot abstractive news summarization. In *The 44th International ACM SIGIR Conference on Research and Development in Information Retrieval (SIGIR), 2021*. ACM.

Yukun Zhu, Ryan Kiros, Rich Zemel, Ruslan Salakhutdinov, Raquel Urtasun, Antonio Torralba, and Sanja Fidler. 2015. Aligning books and movies: Towards story-like visual explanations by watching movies and reading books. In *2015 IEEE International Conference on Computer Vision (ICCV)*, pages 19–27.

Yicheng Zou, Bolin Zhu, Xingwu Hu, Tao Gui, and Qi Zhang. 2021. Low-resource dialogue summarization with domain-agnostic multi-source pretraining. In *Proceedings of the 2021 Conference on Empirical Methods in Natural Language Processing*, pages 80–91, Online and Punta Cana, Dominican Republic. Association for Computational Linguistics.

Knowledge Transfer with Visual Prompt in Multi-modal Dialogue Understanding and Generation

Minjun Zhu[1,2]*, Yixuan Weng[1]*, Bin Li[3], Shizhu He[1,2], Kang Liu[1,2], Jun Zhao[1,2]
[1] National Laboratory of Pattern Recognition, Institute of Automation, CAS
[2] School of Artificial Intelligence, University of Chinese Academy of Sciences
[3] College of Electrical and Information Engineering, Hunan University
zhuminjun2020@ia.ac.cn, wengsyx@gmail.com, libincn@hnu.edu.cn,
{shizhu.he, kliu, jzhao}@nlpr.ia.ac.cn

Abstract

Visual Dialogue (VD) task has recently received increasing attention in AI research. VD aims to generate multi-round, interactive responses based on the dialog history and image content. Existing textual dialogue models cannot fully understand visual information, resulting in a lack of scene features when communicating with humans continuously. Therefore, how to efficiently fuse multi-modal data features remains to be a challenge. In this work, we propose a knowledge transfer method with visual prompt (**VPTG**) fusing multi-modal data, which is a flexible module that can utilize the text-only seq2seq model to handle VD tasks. The VPTG conducts text-image co-learning and multi-modal information fusion with visual prompts and visual knowledge distillation. Specifically, we construct visual prompts from visual representations and then induce sequence-to-sequence (seq2seq) models to fuse visual information and textual contexts by visual-text patterns. Moreover, we also realize visual knowledge transfer through distillation between two different models' text representations, so that the seq2seq model can actively learn visual semantic representations. Extensive experiments on the multi-modal dialogue understanding and generation (MDUG) datasets show the proposed VPTG outperforms other single-modal methods, which demonstrate the effectiveness of visual prompt and visual knowledge transfer.

1 Introduction

Cross-modal understanding between vision and language has become a challenging field in natural language processing and computer vision. With the rapid development of deep neural networks, researchers have made rapid progress in a series of visual language tasks, including moment localization with natural language (Zhang et al., 2019a, 2020; Tan et al., 2021; Li et al., 2022b), image captioning (Vinyals et al., 2015; Chen et al., 2017; Anderson et al., 2017), visual question answering (Tang et al., 2018; Chen et al., 2020; Sheng et al., 2021), etc. The visual dialogue task (Das et al., 2017) aims to perform multiple rounds of interactive dialogue based on dialogue history and image content.

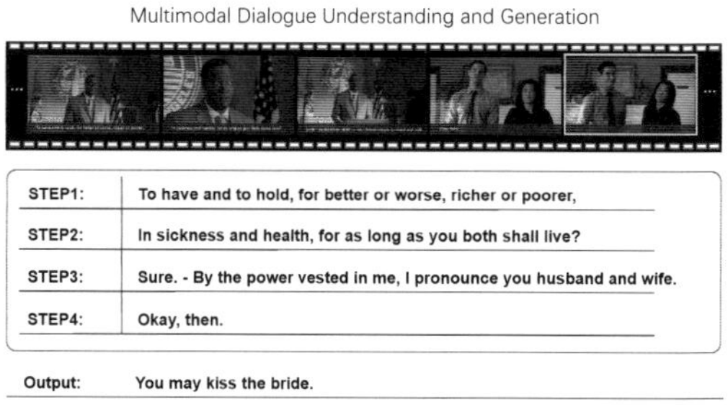

Figure 1: Description of the Multi-modal Dialogue Understanding and Generation (MDUG) task. From step1 to step 3, the video is about a priest, and the subtitles are snippets of wedding vows. For the response generation of step 4, supposing that only dialogue text context was taken, the previous dialog text: "OK, then" is inadequate for generating the expected output: "you may kiss the bride."

Dialogues with multi-modal contexts (visual and textual) are becoming more and more general in daily life (Baltrušaitis et al., 2018), such as communicating messenger tools (e.g. Facebook, WeChat). Compared with visual question answering, Visual Dialogue (VD) tasks not only require answering questions according to visual information but also require a deep understanding of multiple rounds of historical dialogues (Schwartz et al., 2019b; Gan et al., 2019; Chen et al., 2022). In the visual dialogue task, researchers have put forward a lot of relevant datasets, the *GuessWhat?!* (de Vries et al., 2016) and the *Visdial* (Das et al., 2017) set up visual dialog data sets for images. The MDUG (Wang et al., 2022b) is based on video scenes to generate coherent textual responses.

*These authors contributed to this paper equally.

Proceedings of the 29th International Conference on Computational Linguistic, pages 8–19
October 12–17, 2022.

In this work, we mainly focus on video visual dialogue such as the Multi-modal Dialogue Understanding and Generation (MDUG) dataset (Wang et al., 2022b). Compared to image captioning and image visual dialogue, it requires modeling long-distance image sequences, which is more challenging and practical. The MDUG task proposes a multi-modal dialogue task in the video field. It needs the system to generate a response of the current frame based on multi-modal video scene and historical dialogue information, where historical video clips frame and text captions are mapped one-to-one. The video clips and visual images have much abundant and useful information about the plot development. It is easy to pick up on their movements and expressions from visual information. For example, in the last frame of Figure 1. On the one hand, from the body movements of people such as they gradually face each other and a smile on the man's face, we can observe that the man is going to kiss his bride, so models can infer the "kiss" action in generated response. On the other hand, from the wedding vows context, it's easy to infer their roles as bride and groom. Therefore, this example demonstrates the importance of combining images and texts for the MDUG task.

Although much attention has been drawn to dialogue tasks (Das et al., 2017), neural models have shown impressive performance gains in textual dialogue tasks. But existing text-only dialogue methods still have limitations in handling video dialogue tasks in multi-modal scenarios, which may hinder further advancement in this direction. In text-only dialogue tasks, more and more text generation models are pre-trained in the large-scale corpora with the development of pre-trained language models (Brown et al., 2020; Shao et al., 2021). Most of the dialogue pre-training models are based on transformers through pre-training in large-scale dialogue texts and using a large number of encoder and decoder layers (Gu et al., 2022; Zhou et al., 2021; Bao et al., 2021). This can improve the consistency between the generated context and context and the fluency of the generated text. But the bigger challenge is based on the non-homogeneity of the input text-image multi-modal information and the output text information besides challenges in the text-only task in multi-modal dialogue generation tasks.

How to understand and integrate the multi-modal information, and comprehensively perform text generation remains to be an unsolved and important problem. Many efforts have been made to realize a reliable and accurate multi-modal dialogue understanding and generation in similar tasks such as image captioning and video question answering (Fukui et al., 2016; Sharma et al., 2020; Das et al., 2017; Shrestha et al., 2019). However, the methods adopted in that work cannot be directly generalized to the video visual dialogue task, and the video visual dialogue task requires multi-level modeling in a large number of sequence images and dialog history at the same time (Schwartz et al., 2019a).

To take a significant step in this direction and fully utilize seq2seq models' capability, we propose a Visual Prompt Text Generate (**VPTG**) method that can directly provide visual assistance training for multi-modal language models to tackle the above challenges. The VPTG framework can efficiently generate dialogue response that is coherent to both visual images and text dialogue. To model text-image mapping in the same representation space, we adopt CLIP contrastive training to conduct co-learning of image-caption pairs through a pre-trained language model (Liu et al., 2021a). We also use the visual prompt to fuse image visual information into text features. In the training stage, we input the "image" and "answer text" into the CLIP (Radford et al., 2021), and input the "image" feature vector as a visual prompt into the seq2seq model. In addition, to improve the visual modeling ability of language models, we conduct visual knowledge transfer by transferring visual representations to visual prompt and using it to prompt the seq2seq model modeling multi-modal data. Specifically, the "answer text" feature is also provided to the encoder output "[CLS]" vector of the seq2seq model for distillation. We also ask the sequence-to-sequence (seq2seq) model to actively learn visual semantic representations. For efficient training, we adopt an end-to-end training architecture.

In the prediction stage, we only use the image as the input of the CLIP and get the visual prompt, and then perform multi-level learning from visual information to textual information. In the VPTG, we perform efficient representation, co-learning, and fusion of multi-modal information. Extensive experimental results show that the VPTG method consistently outperforms all baseline schemes in the MDUG task, showing the effective ability of the method to make better use of textual and visual information to generate high-quality multi-modal dialogue responses.

In summary, our contributions are as follows:

- In this work, we focus on the video visual dialogue task. To the best of our knowledge, this is the very first attempt to apply the visual prompt for solving the video dialogue response generation task.
- We present a useful method, which can be used in almost all seq2seq models. And it conducts visual prompts and visual knowledge transfer to jointly learn images and text, and effectively generate a response. We explore the task with multi-modal information representation, co-learning, and fusion.
- Extensive experiments are performed to examine the effectiveness of the proposed VPTG on the MDUG dataset, in which we achieve state-of-the-art performances.

2 Related work

2.1 Visual Dialogue Task

With the progress of human-robot interaction technology, more and more dialogue tasks emphasize user-friendliness and ethical safety (Zhang and Zhao, 2021). A dialogue system mainly includes two parts: (1) understanding the history of dialogue; (2) Response in natural language.

The Visual Dialogue (VD) task require agents to have meaningful dialogue with humans in multimodal scenes (Das et al., 2017; Dalu et al., 2019; Li et al., 2021; Wang et al., 2022b). It is more complex than traditional visual tasks (such as Object Detection (Ren et al., 2015), Image Retrieval (Kalantidis et al., 2015)). In the VD task, given some frame or a video clip, a dialog history context, the agent has to ground in image and text, infer context from history, and generate text response accurately. It requires multi-dimensional modeling based on visual information to generate accurate descriptions, which has been used to help visually impaired people better understand the visual content of the environment. The **MDUG** dataset is a VD dataset that aims to generate an interactive response based on the image captions context history and video clips image content. The traditional multi-modal fusion method first uses the visual model to extract the image features and then uses the neural network such as LSTM (Hochreiter and Schmidhuber, 1997) to fuse the information between different modes. In recent years, many methods have been committed to more comprehensive information fusion (Vinyals et al., 2014), such as MHCIAE (Lu et al., 2017) used discriminative learning to migrate knowledge into dialogue generation. ReDAN (Gan et al., 2019) conducted visual dialogue through multi-step reasoning. UTC (Chen et al., 2022) unified the discriminative and generation of Visual Dialogue tasks based on the framework of contrastive learning. Different from previous works, the **VPTG** adopts a more flexible and widely applicable framework that can be integrated with various single-modal pre-trained language models to learn vision-language interactions by taking visual prompt and visual knowledge transfer, which deeply captures the relations between image and texts to mutually reinforce dialogue response generation.

2.2 Pre-Trained Language Model

There are also pre-trained models promising in the visual-language field (Murahari et al., 2019; Wang et al., 2020; Ye et al., 2022). Most of the popular approaches employ an encoder-decoder architecture for visual dialog. The encoder aims at encoding the image and text to fused features, and two separate decoders are employed for ranking and generating respectively. Among them, a variety of attention mechanism-based approaches are proposed to learn the interactions between the image, the answers, and the dialog history in the discriminative setting. The 3D ConvNet was pre-trained on the Kinetics dataset (Carreira and Zisserman, 2017). The CLIP (Radford et al., 2021) and Wenlan (Huo et al., 2021) models are image-text pair pretrained models, which are pre-trained by learning to map text and image to the same vector space. The OFA (Wang et al., 2022a) is a unified model adopting multi-modality pre-training with multi-tasking training objectives. It transforms all multi-modal tasks into sequence-to-sequence (seq2seq) tasks, which realizes the state-of-the-art performance in multiple visual-language tasks.

2.3 Prompt Tuning

How to make better use of pre-trained models has become a concerning problem (Han et al., 2021b). Prompt tuning is a new NLP paradigm used to solve the downstream tasks of the pre-trained model.In the field of multi-modality, increasing methods adopt prompt tuning to learn the aligned features between different modalities. CPT (Yao et al.,

2022) uses color (visual feature) as a bridge to recover masked tokens from cross-modal content, narrowing the gap between pre-training and downstream tasks. The VPTSL (Li et al., 2022a) formulates the natural language video localization task as an extraction reading comprehension task by introducing the discrete visual prompt. And, it implements a new state-of-the-art on the MedVidQA (Gupta et al., 2022) datasets.

The VPTG solves the defect of incomplete utilization of visual features. It also performs visual prediction tasks by $\mathcal{L}_{\mathrm{KL}}$ compared with these prompt methods. This can make the model more fully understand the visual semantics, so as to better multi-modal modeling.

3 Datasets

The multi-modal Dialogue Understanding and Generation task (Wang et al., 2022b) is required to generate a dialogue agent for the next sentence based on the multi-modal scene and the previous dialogue process. This task needs to model the semantics of the session and the scenario of the session. The task provides the multi-modal video of dialogue content and scene. Its ultimate goal is to generate agent replies that meet the context and are related to the video scene.

The videos and dialogues for this task are crawled from online TV series. The dataset is split into a training set, a validation set, and a test set. Each example includes a dialogue session as well as the associated video clip, which is a sequence of frames. The frames from the videos have been downsampled to 3fps.

It is composed of 43,895 videos with 1,100,242 utterances. Each video has an average of 25.07 utterances. We follow the official data split, where 1,000,079, 50,032, and 50,131 utterances are used for training, validation, and testing, respectively.

4 The Proposed Method

We propose the visual prompt Text Generate (VPTG) framework for the multi-modal Dialogue Understanding and Generation (MDUG) task, whose ultimate goal is to generate a response that is coherent to the dialogue context and relevant to the video context. The Figure 2 illustrates the architecture of VPTG. It is challenging to directly generate the dialogue response according to multi-modal data. To tackle this challenge of data alignment and fusion between image and text, we split the MDUG task into two simultaneous modules: (1) the visual predictor module is first used to generate **visual prompt** (Section 4.1) by jointly training an image encoder and a text encoder and fusion image information into a text representation. (2) The text predictor conducts **Visual Knowledge Transfer** (Section 4.2) to guarantee response generation with information alignment between text and image.

4.1 Visual Prompt

The visual prompt method was proposed in the Visual Predictor module. In this module, we aim at learning multi-modal feature representation and constructing visual prompts to reinforce semantic modeling.

In the MDUG task, an example includes a dialogue session and the associated video clip which is a sequence of frames (3 frames per second). In the VPTG, we input the last frame of video I and a corresponding next textual response T corresponding at a time. Because image and text are heterogeneous data, we leverage the CLIP (Radford et al., 2021) to model joint representations of image and text. For multi-modal data, joint representations are projected to the same space using all of the modalities as input. The CLIP (Radford et al., 2021) is a visual-language pre-training model that learns both visual and language representations by predicting the correct pairings of a batch of {image, text} training examples. In our model, for the current frame image and the next textual response, we utilize an image encoder to get visual prompt $\mathcal{V}_{\text{image}} \in \mathbb{R}^k$ and a text encoder to get $V_{\text{text}} \in \mathbb{R}^k$, they are jointly trained to respectively map the input image and text into a unified representation space. We adopt contrastive learning as its training objective. We use L_{CL} to close the semantic distance of image-text pairs, where ground truth image-text pairs are regarded as positive samples $\mathbf{X}^+ = \{\mathbf{x}_i^+\}_{i=1}^n$, and mismatched image-text pairs constructed as negative ones $\mathbf{X}^- = \{\mathbf{x}_i^-\}_{i=1}^m$.

$$L_{CL} = -\sum_{i=0}^{n}\left[\log \frac{\operatorname{Sim}(x_i,x_i^+)}{\operatorname{Sim}(x_i,x_i^+)+\sum_{j=1}^{m}\operatorname{Sim}(x_i,x_j^-)}\right]$$
$$\operatorname{Sim}(x_i,x_j) = \exp\left(f(x_i)^T f(x_j)\right) \tag{1}$$

4.1.1 Prompt Designing

The information coming from text and image modalities may have varying predictive power and noise topology (Baltrušaitis et al., 2018). After learning joint representations of image-text pairs,

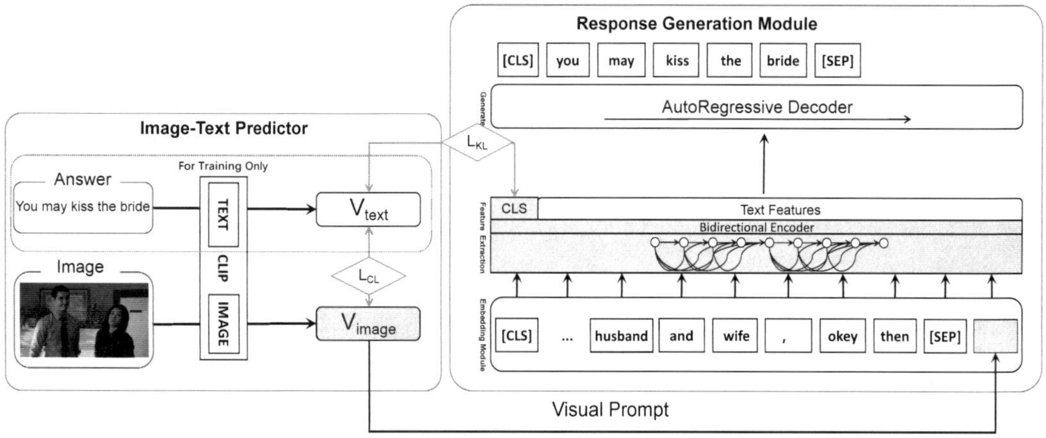

Figure 2: The architecture of the proposed method. In the training stage, we input the "image" and "answer text" into two separate encoders of CLIP, and input the image feature vector as a visual prompt into the seq2seq model. In addition, the answer eigenvector is also provided to the encoder output "[CLS]" vector of the seq2seq model for distillation. In the prediction stage, we only use the image as the input of the CLIP and get the visual prompt.

we conduct visual prompt learning. Unlike traditional visual prompt Tuning methods aiming to finetune large-scale Transformer modules with a small amount of task-specific learnable parameters, we construct the visual prompt to fuse visual modality into text modeling and generation, which can also be trained end-to-end.

We adopt the visual image representation as the visual token for prompting the pre-trained language model. Specifically, the image representation V_{image} was transferred to the same dimension as the input text tokens as a visual prompt.

$$\mathcal{P}_{\text{t}} = Linear(\mathcal{V}_{\text{image}}) \tag{2}$$

where $\mathbf{P}_{\text{t}} \in \mathbb{R}^d$,d is the dimension of text predictor encoder embedding; $Linear$ is a single feed-forward layer.

4.1.2 Prompt Tuning

Intuitively, the visual prompt $\mathcal{P}_{\text{t}}$ is used as the visual token which concatenates with the text dialogue sentence and the last video frame image. The "[CLS]" is positioned at the head of the input token, while the prompt $\mathcal{P}_{\text{t}}$ is used as the trigger to model and generate a response. After concatenation, the embedding module is adopted for learning the features in the same vector space. On the one hand, the visual prompt covers the non-verbal part that the text token lacks. On the other head, the visual prompt is supervised by the visual frames, where some visual features can be the extra knowledge for the pre-trained model when fine-tuning.

$$\mathbf{P} = \mathbf{Embedded}\left([\text{CLS}]\mathbf{Text}[\text{SEP}]\right)\mathbf{Concat}\mathcal{P}_{\text{t}} \tag{3}$$

4.2 Visual Knowledge Transfer

The text predictor module is based on the seq2seq Transformer model (Vaswani et al., 2017a). The Transformer is Encoder-Decoder architecture, which is proved to be outstanding for text generation. The encoder produces a global contextual representation based on multi-modal representation fusion, and the decoder will use the multi-head attention mechanism to fuse encoder information, and then generate the final frame predicted response token by token. To make information alignment, we propose **Visual knowledge transfer** to distil knowledge by cross-attention. This thought has been proved to perform better multi-modal information fusion in the textual question answering field (Izacard and Grave, 2020).

4.2.1 Text Encoder Distill Learning

In text predictor, each $\mathbf{P}$ constructed in Visual Prompt is given as input to a seq2seq model encoder.

$$V_P = \text{Encoder}_{seq2seq}(\mathbf{P}) \tag{4}$$

Let $V_{CLS}^{seq2seq} \in \mathbb{R}^d$ be the [CLS] token's representation of the encoded query V_P, it models the whole representation containing dialogue text and visual prompt in the bidirectional encoder. We will assume that the last hidden state output among two encoders and text can be defined as $p_1(t \mid p)$ and $p_2(t \mid z)$. There are two transformer encoders in the VPTG, where we call the visual predictor encoder as $\mathbf{Encoder}_1$, the text predictor encoder as $\mathbf{Encoder}_2$.

$$p_1(t \mid p) \propto V_{text}^{CLIP}, \quad p_2(t \mid z) \propto V_{CLS}^{seq2seq} \quad (5)$$

where t is input dialogue text, p is the input frame image; z is the visual prompt according to p; $V_{text}^{CLIP} \in \mathbb{R}^k$ is the representation of image in the visual predictor. The p_1 represent the $\mathbf{Encoder}_1$, and the p_2 represent the $\mathbf{Encoder}_2$. We close the gap between $V_{CLS}^{seq2seq}$ and V_{text}^{CLIP} by minimizing the KL-divergence. This aims at training the response generator ($\mathbf{Encoder}_2$) with visual knowledge information from the image-text predictor ($\mathbf{Encoder}_1$).

$$\begin{aligned} \mathcal{L}_{\mathrm{KL}}^0(\theta, \mathcal{P}_{\mathrm{t}}) &= D_{KL}(V_{CLS}^{seq2seq}(x) \| w_0 V_{text}^{CLIP}(x)) \\ \mathcal{L}_{\mathrm{KL}}^1(\theta, \mathcal{P}_{\mathrm{t}}) &= D_{KL}(w_0 V_{text}^{CLIP}(x) \| V_{CLS}^{seq2seq}(x)) \\ \mathcal{L}_{\mathrm{KL}}(\theta, \mathcal{P}_{\mathrm{t}}) &= \frac{1}{2} \sum_{x \in \mathcal{X}} \left(\mathcal{L}_{\mathrm{KL}}^0(\theta, \mathcal{P}_{\mathrm{t}}) + \mathcal{L}_{\mathrm{KL}}^1(\theta, \mathcal{P}_{\mathrm{t}})\right) \end{aligned} \quad (6)$$

where $\mathcal{X}$ is the training set of all image-text pairs. $w_0 \in \mathbb{R}^{d \times k}$ is a trainable weights vector. The text predictor encoder ($\mathbf{Encoder}_2$) is trained simultaneously by the response generation task. We take the formula above to perform visual knowledge distill learning. In training $\mathcal{L}_{\mathrm{KL}}$, it performs gradient decoupling (stop-gradient operator) for $V_{text}^{CLIP}(x)$ and $\mathbf{Encoder}_1$. This visual knowledge distill learning method requires the seq2seq model (or $\mathbf{Encoder}_2$) to actively learn visual semantic representation, so as to increase the model's perception of visual signals and avoid ignoring information of visual prompt.

4.2.2 Response Generation

Finally, we generate responses with the seq2seq model's decoder. We define L_{gen} as the autoregressive loss.

$$L_{gen} = -\sum_{n=1}^{N} p(y_i) \log \frac{\exp(y_i)}{\sum_{n=1}^{N} \exp(y_i)} \quad (7)$$

where y_i is the i-th generated token by the language model. N is the size of the target vocabulary.

4.3 Training and Inference

Combining the above derivations, our training objective that we seek to minimize for response becomes:

$$\mathcal{L} = \mathcal{L}_{\mathrm{KL}} + \lambda \mathcal{L}_{gen} + \gamma \mathcal{L}_{CL}, \gamma \in \mathbb{R}, \lambda \in \mathbb{R}. \quad (8)$$

We jointly train the visual predictor and text predictor as an end-to-end training approach.

For inference, we first encode the input image-text pairs by the visual predictor, then construct the visual prompt to fuse multi-modal representation. The text predictor can generate predicted responses after concatenation between the text tokens and the visual token.

5 Experiments

In this section, we will introduce the evaluation indicators and experimental settings. Then we compare VPTG with the existing dialogue generation technology and ablation experiments to prove the effectiveness of our method.

5.1 Evaluation Metrics

Following prior work (Chen et al., 2015; Laokulrat et al., 2016; Pasunuru and Bansal, 2017; Liu et al., 2021b), we use a variety of evaluation indicators, which can evaluate the generation quality of sentence level and word level at the same time, and show the detailed performance of the system more comprehensively. We adopt "BLEU" (Papineni et al., 2002), "ROUGE" (Lin, 2004), "METEOR" (Denkowski and Lavie, 2014) and "CIDER" (Vedantam et al., 2015) as the evaluation metrics, which can assess the quality of visual dialogue generation, including fidelity and diversity.

5.2 Implementation Details

In order to compare the functions of the system more fairly, we follow the setting of the baseline scheme and only compare whether to add the VPTG module. In recent years, natural language processing significant progress has been achieved (Han et al., 2021a; Qiu et al., 2020) due to the introduction of Pre-trained Language Model (Peters et al., 2018; Devlin et al., 2019; Radford and Narasimhan, 2018). Therefore, more and more methods begin to introduce the pre-trained language model in the dialogue generation task (Zhang et al., 2019b; Adiwardana et al., 2020; Roller et al., 2021b; Thoppilan et al., 2022; Gu et al., 2022).

For all methods, we use the same CLIP [1] (Radford et al., 2021) model as feature extraction It

[1] `https://huggingface.co/openai/clip-vit-base-patch32`

Models		BLEU-1	ROUGE-L	METEOR	CIDEr	Avg
Random Mode		4.81	3.92	2.21	2.42	3.34
BART-base(Lewis et al., 2019) (2019)	Originally	5.02	4.35	2.54	3.75	3.92
	Fintune	5.74	6.10	3.87	4.11	4.96
	With VPTG	**6.12**	**6.52**	**4.01**	**4.35**	**5.25(0.29↑)**
T5-base (2020)	Originally	2.78	4.21	2.33	**1.20**	2.63
	Fintune	2.94	4.44	2.81	0.58	2.69
	With VPTG	**3.24**	**5.12**	**2.98**	0.89	**3.06(0.37↑)**
Blender-400M (Roller et al., 2021a)(2021)	Originally	6.03	7.69	5.43	3.51	5.67
	Fintune	7.01	8.73	6.05	5.85	6.91
	With VPTG	**7.55**	**9.15**	**6.49**	**6.61**	**7.45(0.54↑)**

Table 1: Performance comparison of the variants methods on MDUG dataset. We highlight the best score in each column in **bold**, and the second best score with underline. We also show the improvement between first place and second place.

Case Study	BLEU-1	ROUGE-L	METEOR	CIDEr	Avg
Baseline	7.01	8.73	6.05	5.85	6.91
W/O $\mathcal{L}_{\text{KL}}$	7.25	8.91	6.24	7.12	7.38
W/O Visual-Feature	7.10	8.79	6.34	6.01	7.06
W/O visual prompt	6.45	8.10	5.78	5.62	6.49
VPTG	**7.55**	**9.15**	**6.49**	**6.61**	**7.45**

Table 2: We conduct the ablation study to analyze the performance of the VPTG on the Blender-400M model, where we use the same parameters to train the model and report the highest score.

has 8 attention heads and 12 layers, and its hidden size is 512. For the seq2seq model, we all use the base size model for testing. And for the remaining settings, we follow the original code.

We train the model using the Pytorch[2] (Paszke et al., 2019) on the NVIDIA RTX3090 GPU and use the hugging-face[3] (Wolf et al., 2020) framework. We use the AdamW (Loshchilov and Hutter, 2018) as the optimizer and the learning rate is set to 1e-5 with the warm-up (He et al., 2016). The batch size is 24. We set the maximum length of 512 (we set the max length as 128 for Blender, because it supports up to 128 lengths of input), and deleted the excess. We use the linear decay of the learning rate and gradient clipping of 1e-6. The dropout (Srivastava et al., 2014) of 0.1 is applied to prevent overfitting. The detailed experimental settings are shown in **Table 1**.

All hyperparameters are optimized on the Valid set. In all our experiments, at the end of each training phase, we will test the effective data set and select the highest model (mainly depending on BLEU) in the test data set for prediction. We report the results in the test data set. We repeated the experiment three times and reported the average score.

[2] https://pytorch.org

[3] https://github.com/huggingface/transformers

5.3 Comparison with State-of-the-Art Methods

In the MDUG dataset, we compared the baseline scheme with the existing dialogue generation.

BART (Lewis et al., 2019) uses a standard seq2seq transformer (Vaswani et al., 2017b) structure. Its structure is very simple, which can be seen as a combination of BERT (Devlin et al., 2018) and GPT (Radford and Narasimhan, 2018). In the pre-training stage, it destroys the original text by randomly disrupting the order of the original sentences and adding mask tags. After that, the BART (Lewis et al., 2019) reconstructs the original text by denoising it. The BART (Lewis et al., 2019) achieves the best performance in translation and summary tasks that need to be generated.

T5 treats all tasks as text-to-text tasks. It is different from the BART (Lewis et al., 2019) in that the pre-training stage only requires the decoder to recover the masked part without full-text recovery. It has even surpassed the human level in many natural language tasks (Wang et al., 2018, 2019).

Blender (Roller et al., 2021a) is a pre-training model in the chat field. It carries out pre-training in a large number of dialogues, which improves the dialogue fluency of the model. It can provide users with interesting chat preferences, display personality, and so on. Blender can maintain consistent personality attributes in the dialogue and surpasses the existing models in terms of participation and

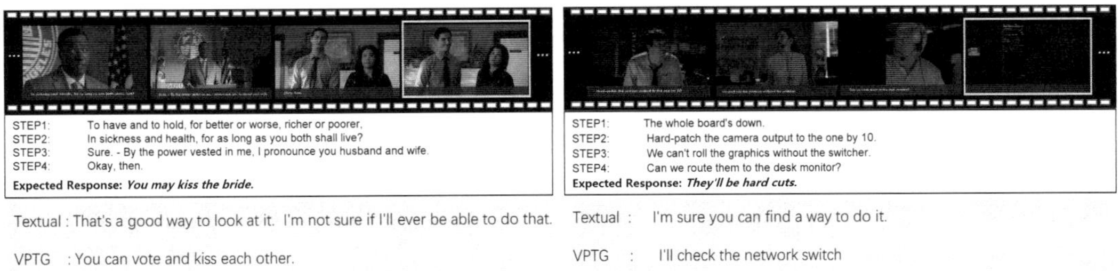

Figure 3: Examples of the generated results.

humanization indicators.

5.4 Experimental Result

We report the performance of the model in **Table 2**. The "Originally" refers to the use of the original pre-training model for a zero-shot generation. The "Finetune" means that we fine-tune the data set and select the highest score to test in the test. The "With VPTG" means that we have modified the structure of the model and added the VPTG module based on the existing language model, which enables us to give the visual ability to the language model that has never seen an image.

It is not difficult to find that, other models have poor zero-shot effects in the field of dialogue except the Blender. This is because the T5 model and the Bart model are pre-trained in a large-scale general corpus, which is difficult to migrate directly to the field of dialogue. Even if these models are fine-tuned, the effect is still insufficient, even worse than the result of random selection. This shows that Visual Dialogue tasks have strong open attributes and need to use more features.

After the VPTG is added to the model, the CLIP can provide visual semantic features. This makes the seq2seq model have a more comprehensive perceptual performance. It can analyze the overall scene and generate dialogue text more in line with the scene. In the "With VPTG" of Table 1, the performance of all models has been significantly improved. This shows the effectiveness of the VPTG module.

5.5 Ablation Study

In **Table 3**, we can see some performance comparisons. We further carry out care learning in Blender (Roller et al., 2021a), which is the best pre-trained model in MDUG tasks (Wang et al., 2022b). It can fully show the effect differences brought by different methods.

First, we try to cancel the $\mathcal{L}_{\text{KL}}$ loss, which means that we no longer require the model to predict the actual video scene. This may lead to the lack of understanding of the scene in the model so that the generated text lacks the modelling of the scene.

After cancelling the visual feature, we will no longer provide the video feature vector of the current scene. This may make the model lack visual semantic features and cause the omission of environmental scenes.

We tested the use of dot products to integrate visual features into the embedding matrix of the seq2seq model, but the effects decreased significantly. We believe that if we do not use the visual prompt to provide visual features, the direct dot product will cause the catastrophic forgetting problem of the pre-training language model. It will destroy the original semantic understanding ability of the pre-training language model and become a kind of noise interference through the fusion of direct dot product feature vectors.

5.6 Case Study

In Figure 3, we select two examples to show. We can see that the VPTG model can better model scene information and generate text with specific visual semantics than the single modal language pre-training model. Compared with the single model, the VPTG has higher fluency in the field of dialogue. This fully shows that the VPTG can deeply mine visual signals.

6 Conclusions

In this paper, we proposed a new visual knowledge fusing paradigm that provides the pre-trained language generation model with the visual prompt. The VPTG module is flexible and can support almost all seq2seq models to be used in multi-modal dialogue generation tasks. It realizes the language model's understanding of visual information by transforming visual features into embedding prompts. We have conducted vast experiments on the task of multi-modal Dialogue Understanding and Generation. The VPTG outperforms all other baselines in MDUG tasks for these experiments, which reflects the effectiveness of the proposed method.

References

Daniel Adiwardana, Minh-Thang Luong, David R. So, Jamie Hall, Noah Fiedel, Romal Thoppilan, Zi Yang, Apoorv Kulshreshtha, Gaurav Nemade, Yifeng Lu, and Quoc V. Le. 2020. Towards a human-like open-domain chatbot. *arXiv: Computation and Language.*

Peter Anderson, Xiaodong He, Chris Buehler, Damien Teney, Mark Johnson, Stephen Gould, and Lei Zhang. 2017. Bottom-up and top-down attention for image captioning and visual question answering. *computer vision and pattern recognition.*

Tadas Baltrušaitis, Chaitanya Ahuja, and Louis-Philippe Morency. 2018. Multimodal machine learning: A survey and taxonomy. *IEEE transactions on pattern analysis and machine intelligence*, 41(2):423–443.

Siqi Bao, Huang He, Fan Wang, Hua Wu, Haifeng Wang, Wenquan Wu, Zhihua Wu, Zhen Guo, Hua Lu, Xinxian Huang, Xin Tian, Xu Xinchao, Yingzhan Lin, and Zheng-Yu Niu. 2021. Plato-xl: Exploring the large-scale pre-training of dialogue generation. *arXiv: Computation and Language.*

Tom Brown, Benjamin Mann, Nick Ryder, Melanie Subbiah, Jared D Kaplan, Prafulla Dhariwal, Arvind Neelakantan, Pranav Shyam, Girish Sastry, Amanda Askell, Sandhini Agarwal, Ariel Herbert-Voss, Gretchen Krueger, Tom Henighan, Rewon Child, Aditya Ramesh, Daniel Ziegler, Jeffrey Wu, Clemens Winter, Chris Hesse, Mark Chen, Eric Sigler, Mateusz Litwin, Scott Gray, Benjamin Chess, Jack Clark, Christopher Berner, Sam McCandlish, Alec Radford, Ilya Sutskever, and Dario Amodei. 2020. Language models are few-shot learners. In *Advances in Neural Information Processing Systems*, volume 33, pages 1877–1901. Curran Associates, Inc.

Joao Carreira and Andrew Zisserman. 2017. Quo vadis, action recognition? a new model and the kinetics dataset. In *Computer Vision and Pattern Recognition.*

Cheng Chen, Yudong Zhu, Zhenshan Tan, Qingrong Cheng, Xin Jiang, Qun Liu, and Xiaodong Gu. 2022. Utc: A unified transformer with inter-task contrastive learning for visual dialog.

Long Chen, Xin Yan, Jun Xiao, Hanwang Zhang, Shiliang Pu, and Yueting Zhuang. 2020. Counterfactual samples synthesizing for robust visual question answering. *computer vision and pattern recognition.*

Long Chen, Hanwang Zhang, Jun Xiao, Liqiang Nie, Jian Shao, Wei Liu, and Tat-Seng Chua. 2017. Sca-cnn: Spatial and channel-wise attention in convolutional networks for image captioning. *computer vision and pattern recognition.*

Xinlei Chen, Hao Fang, Tsung-Yi Lin, Ramakrishna Vedantam, Saurabh Gupta, Piotr Dollár, and C. Lawrence Zitnick. 2015. Microsoft COCO captions: Data collection and evaluation server. *CoRR*, abs/1504.00325.

Guo Dalu, Xu Chang, and Tao Dacheng. 2019. Image-question-answer synergistic network for visual dialog. *computer vision and pattern recognition.*

Abhishek Das, Satwik Kottur, Khushi Gupta, Avi Singh, Deshraj Yadav, Jose M. F. Moura, Devi Parikh, and Dhruv Batra. 2017. Visual dialog. *computer vision and pattern recognition.*

Harm de Vries, Florian Strub, Sarath Chandar, Olivier Pietquin, Hugo Larochelle, and Aaron Courville. 2016. Guesswhat?! visual object discovery through multi-modal dialogue. *computer vision and pattern recognition.*

Michael Denkowski and Alon Lavie. 2014. Meteor universal: Language specific translation evaluation for any target language. In *Proceedings of the Ninth Workshop on Statistical Machine Translation*, pages 376–380, Baltimore, Maryland, USA. Association for Computational Linguistics.

Jacob Devlin, Ming-Wei Chang, Kenton Lee, and Kristina Toutanova. 2018. Bert: Pre-training of deep bidirectional transformers for language understanding. *north american chapter of the association for computational linguistics.*

Jacob Devlin, Ming-Wei Chang, Kenton Lee, and Kristina Toutanova. 2019. BERT: Pre-training of deep bidirectional transformers for language understanding. In *Proceedings of the 2019 Conference of the North American Chapter of the Association for Computational Linguistics: Human Language Technologies, Volume 1 (Long and Short Papers)*, pages 4171–4186, Minneapolis, Minnesota. Association for Computational Linguistics.

Akira Fukui, Dong Huk Park, Daylen Yang, Anna Rohrbach, Trevor Darrell, and Marcus Rohrbach. 2016. Multimodal compact bilinear pooling for visual question answering and visual grounding. *empirical methods in natural language processing.*

Zhe Gan, Yu Cheng, Ahmed El Kholy, Linjie Li, Jingjing Liu, and Jianfeng Gao. 2019. Multi-step reasoning via recurrent dual attention for visual dialog. *meeting of the association for computational linguistics.*

Yuxian Gu, Jiaxin Wen, Hao Sun, Yi Song, Pei Ke, Chujie Zheng, Zheng Zhang, Jianzhu Yao, Xiaoyan Zhu, Jie Tang, and Minlie Huang. 2022. Eva2.0: Investigating open-domain chinese dialogue systems with large-scale pre-training.

Deepak Gupta, Kush Attal, and Dina Demner-Fushman. 2022. A Dataset for Medical Instructional Video Classification and Question Answering. *arXiv preprint arXiv:2201.12888*.

Xu Han, Zhengyan Zhang, Ning Ding, Yuxian Gu, Xiao Liu, Yuqi Huo, Jiezhong Qiu, Yuan Yao, Ao Zhang, Liang Zhang, Wentao Han, Minlie Huang, Qin Jin, Yanyan Lan, Yang Liu, Zhiyuan Liu, Zhiwu Lu, Xipeng Qiu, Ruihua Song, Jie Tang, Ji-Rong Wen, Jinhui Yuan, Wayne Xin Zhao, and Jun Zhu. 2021a. Pre-trained models: Past, present and future. *AI Open*, 2:225–250.

Xu Han, Zhengyan Zhang, Ning Ding, Yuxian Gu, Xiao Liu, Yuqi Huo, Jiezhong Qiu, Liang Zhang, Wentao Han, Minlie Huang, Qin Jin, Yanyan Lan, Yang Liu, Zhiyuan Liu, Zhiwu Lu, Xipeng Qiu, Ruihua Song, Jie Tang, Ji-Rong Wen, Jinhui Yuan, Wayne Xin Zhao, and Jun Zhu. 2021b. Pre-trained models: Past, present and future. *AI Open*.

Kaiming He, Xiangyu Zhang, Shaoqing Ren, and Jian Sun. 2016. Deep residual learning for image recognition. In *2016 IEEE Conference on Computer Vision and Pattern Recognition (CVPR)*, pages 770–778.

Sepp Hochreiter and Jürgen Schmidhuber. 1997. Long short-term memory. *Neural Computation*.

Yuqi Huo, Manli Zhang, Guangzhen Liu, Haoyu Lu, Yizhao Gao, Guoxing Yang, Jingyuan Wen, Heng Zhang, Baogui Xu, Weihao Zheng, Zongzheng Xi, Yueqian Yang, Anwen Hu, Jinming Zhao, Ruichen Li, Yida Zhao, Liang Zhang, Yuqing Song, Xin Hong, Wanqing Cui, Dan Yang Hou, Yingyan Li, Junyi Li, Peiyu Liu, Zheng Gong, Chuhao Jin, Yuchong Sun, Shizhe Chen, Zhiwu Lu, Zhicheng Dou, Qin Jin, Yanyan Lan, Wayne Xin Zhao, Ruihua Song, and Ji-Rong Wen. 2021. Wenlan: Bridging vision and language by large-scale multi-modal pre-training. *arXiv: Computer Vision and Pattern Recognition*.

Gautier Izacard and Edouard Grave. 2020. Distilling knowledge from reader to retriever for question answering. *arXiv preprint arXiv:2012.04584*.

Yannis Kalantidis, Clayton Mellina, and Simon Osindero. 2015. Cross-dimensional weighting for aggregated deep convolutional features. *european conference on computer vision*.

Natsuda Laokulrat, Sang Phan, Noriki Nishida, Raphael Shu, Yo Ehara, Naoaki Okazaki, Yusuke Miyao, and Hideki Nakayama. 2016. Generating video description using sequence-to-sequence model with temporal attention. *international conference on computational linguistics*.

Michael Lewis, Yinhan Liu, Naman Goyal, Marjan Ghazvininejad, Abdelrahman Mohamed, Omer Levy, Veselin Stoyanov, and Luke Zettlemoyer. 2019. Bart: Denoising sequence-to-sequence pre-training for natural language generation, translation, and comprehension. *meeting of the association for computational linguistics*.

Bin Li, Yixuan Weng, Bin Sun, and Shutao Li. 2022a. Towards visual-prompt temporal answering grounding in medical instructional video. *arXiv preprint arXiv:2203.06667*.

Bin Li, Yixuan Weng, Fei Xia, Bin Sun, and Shutao Li. 2022b. Vpai_lab at medvidqa 2022: A two-stage cross-modal fusion method for medical instructional video classification. In *Proceedings of the 21st Workshop on Biomedical Language Processing*, pages 212–219.

Zekang Li, Zongjia Li, Jinchao Zhang, Yang Feng, and Jie Zhou. 2021. Bridging text and video: A universal multimodal transformer for audio-visual scene-aware dialog. *IEEE Transactions on Audio, Speech, and Language Processing*.

Chin-Yew Lin. 2004. ROUGE: A package for automatic evaluation of summaries. In *Text Summarization Branches Out*, pages 74–81, Barcelona, Spain. Association for Computational Linguistics.

Pengfei Liu, Weizhe Yuan, Jinlan Fu, Zhengbao Jiang, Hiroaki Hayashi, and Graham Neubig. 2021a. Pre-train, prompt, and predict: A systematic survey of prompting methods in natural language processing. *arXiv: Computation and Language*.

Wei Liu, Sihan Chen, Longteng Guo, Xinxin Zhu, and Jing Liu. 2021b. Cptr: Full transformer network for image captioning. *arXiv: Computer Vision and Pattern Recognition*.

Ilya Loshchilov and Frank Hutter. 2018. Decoupled weight decay regularization. In *International Conference on Learning Representations*.

Jiasen Lu, Anitha Kannan, Jianwei Yang, Devi Parikh, and Dhruv Batra. 2017. Best of both worlds: Transferring knowledge from discriminative learning to a generative visual dialog model. *neural information processing systems*.

Vishvak Murahari, Dhruv Batra, Devi Parikh, and Abhishek Das. 2019. Large-scale pretraining for visual dialog: A simple state-of-the-art baseline. *european conference on computer vision*.

Kishore Papineni, Salim Roukos, Todd Ward, and Wei-Jing Zhu. 2002. Bleu: a method for automatic evaluation of machine translation. In *Proceedings of the 40th Annual Meeting of the Association for Computational Linguistics*, pages 311–318, Philadelphia, Pennsylvania, USA. Association for Computational Linguistics.

Ramakanth Pasunuru and Mohit Bansal. 2017. Reinforced video captioning with entailment rewards. *empirical methods in natural language processing*.

Adam Paszke, Sam Gross, Francisco Massa, Adam Lerer, James Bradbury, Gregory Chanan, Trevor Killeen, Zeming Lin, Natalia Gimelshein, Luca Antiga, Alban Desmaison, Andreas Kopf, Edward

Yang, Zachary DeVito, Martin Raison, Alykhan Tejani, Sasank Chilamkurthy, Benoit Steiner, Lu Fang, Junjie Bai, and Soumith Chintala. 2019. Pytorch: An imperative style, high-performance deep learning library. In *Advances in Neural Information Processing Systems*, volume 32. Curran Associates, Inc.

Matthew E. Peters, Mark Neumann, Mohit Iyyer, Matt Gardner, Christopher Clark, Kenton Lee, and Luke Zettlemoyer. 2018. Deep contextualized word representations. In *North American Chapter of the Association for Computational Linguistics*.

Xipeng Qiu, Tianxiang Sun, Yige Xu, Yunfan Shao, Ning Dai, and Xuanjing Huang. 2020. Pre-trained models for natural language processing: A survey. *CoRR*, abs/2003.08271.

Alec Radford, Jong Wook Kim, Chris Hallacy, Aditya Ramesh, Gabriel Goh, Sandhini Agarwal, Girish Sastry, Amanda Askell, Pamela Mishkin, Jack Clark, Gretchen Krueger, and Ilya Sutskever. 2021. Learning transferable visual models from natural language supervision. In *Proceedings of the 38th International Conference on Machine Learning*, volume 139 of *Proceedings of Machine Learning Research*, pages 8748–8763. PMLR.

Alec Radford and Karthik Narasimhan. 2018. Improving language understanding by generative pretraining.

Shaoqing Ren, Kaiming He, Ross Girshick, and Jian Sun. 2015. Faster r-cnn: Towards real-time object detection with region proposal networks. *IEEE Transactions on Pattern Analysis and Machine Intelligence*.

Stephen Roller, Emily Dinan, Naman Goyal, Da Ju, Mary Williamson, Yinhan Liu, Jing Xu, Myle Ott, Eric Michael Smith, Y-Lan Boureau, and Jason Weston. 2021a. Recipes for building an open-domain chatbot. *conference of the european chapter of the association for computational linguistics*.

Stephen Roller, Emily Dinan, Naman Goyal, Da Ju, Mary Williamson, Yinhan Liu, Jing Xu, Myle Ott, Eric Michael Smith, Y-Lan Boureau, and Jason Weston. 2021b. Recipes for building an open-domain chatbot. In *Proceedings of the 16th Conference of the European Chapter of the Association for Computational Linguistics: Main Volume*, pages 300–325, Online. Association for Computational Linguistics.

Idan Schwartz, Alexander G. Schwing, and Tamir Hazan. 2019a. A simple baseline for audio-visual scene-aware dialog. *computer vision and pattern recognition*.

Idan Schwartz, Seunghak Yu, Tamir Hazan, and Alexander G. Schwing. 2019b. Factor graph attention. *computer vision and pattern recognition*.

Yunfan Shao, Zhichao Geng, Yitao Liu, Junqi Dai, Fei Yang, Li Zhe, Hujun Bao, and Xipeng Qiu. 2021. Cpt: A pre-trained unbalanced transformer for both chinese language understanding and generation. *arXiv: Computation and Language*.

Himanshu Sharma, Manmohan Agrahari, Sujeet Kumar Singh, Mohd Firoj, and Ravi Kumar Mishra. 2020. Image captioning: A comprehensive survey. In *2020 International Conference on Power Electronics IoT Applications in Renewable Energy and its Control (PARC)*, pages 325–328.

Sasha Sheng, Amanpreet Singh, Vedanuj Goswami, Jose Alberto Lopez Magana, Wojciech Galuba, Devi Parikh, and Douwe Kiela. 2021. Human-adversarial visual question answering. *arXiv: Computer Vision and Pattern Recognition*.

Robik Shrestha, Kushal Kafle, and Christopher Kanan. 2019. Answer them all! toward universal visual question answering models. *computer vision and pattern recognition*.

Nitish Srivastava, Geoffrey E. Hinton, Alex Krizhevsky, Ilya Sutskever, and Ruslan Salakhutdinov. 2014. Dropout: a simple way to prevent neural networks from overfitting. *Journal of Machine Learning Research*, 15:1929–1958.

Yi Tan, Yanbin Hao, Xiangnan He, Yinwei Wei, and Xun Yang. 2021. Selective dependency aggregation for action classification. *acm multimedia*.

Kaihua Tang, Hanwang Zhang, Baoyuan Wu, Wenhan Luo, and Wei Liu. 2018. Learning to compose dynamic tree structures for visual contexts. *computer vision and pattern recognition*.

Romal Thoppilan, Daniel De Freitas, Jamie Hall, Noam Shazeer, Apoorv Kulshreshtha, Heng-Tze Cheng, Alicia Jin, Taylor Bos, Leslie Baker, Yu Du, YaGuang Li, Hongrae Lee, Huaixiu Steven Zheng, Amin Ghafouri, Marcelo Menegali, Yanping Huang, Maxim Krikun, Dmitry Lepikhin, James Qin, Dehao Chen, Yuanzhong Xu, Zhifeng Chen, Adam Roberts, Maarten Bosma, Yanqi Zhou, Chung-Ching Chang, Igor Krivokon, Will Rusch, Marc Pickett, Kathleen Meier-Hellstern, Meredith Ringel Morris, Tulsee Doshi, Renelito Delos Santos, Toju Duke, Johnny Soraker, Ben Zevenbergen, Vinodkumar Prabhakaran, Mark Diaz, Ben Hutchinson, Kristen Olson, Alejandra Molina, Erin Hoffman-John, Josh Lee, Lora Aroyo, Ravi Rajakumar, Alena Butryna, Matthew Lamm, Viktoriya Kuzmina, Joe Fenton, Aaron Cohen, Rachel Bernstein, Ray Kurzweil, Blaise Aguera-Arcas, Claire Cui, Marian Croak, Ed Chi, and Quoc Le. 2022. Lamda: Language models for dialog applications.

Ashish Vaswani, Noam Shazeer, Niki Parmar, Jakob Uszkoreit, Llion Jones, Aidan N. Gomez, Lukasz Kaiser, and Illia Polosukhin. 2017a. Attention is all you need.

Ashish Vaswani, Noam Shazeer, Niki Parmar, Jakob Uszkoreit, Llion Jones, Aidan N. Gomez, Lukasz Kaiser, and Illia Polosukhin. 2017b. Attention is all you need. *neural information processing systems*.

Ramakrishna Vedantam, C. Lawrence Zitnick, and Devi Parikh. 2015. Cider: Consensus-based image description evaluation. In *2015 IEEE Conference on Computer Vision and Pattern Recognition (CVPR)*, pages 4566–4575.

Oriol Vinyals, Alexander Toshev, Samy Bengio, and Dumitru Erhan. 2014. Show and tell: A neural image caption generator. *computer vision and pattern recognition*.

Oriol Vinyals, Alexander Toshev, Samy Bengio, and Dumitru Erhan. 2015. Show and tell: A neural image caption generator. *computer vision and pattern recognition*.

Alex Wang, Yada Pruksachatkun, Nikita Nangia, Amanpreet Singh, Julian Michael, Felix Hill, Omer Levy, and Samuel R. Bowman. 2019. *SuperGLUE: A Stickier Benchmark for General-Purpose Language Understanding Systems*. Curran Associates Inc., Red Hook, NY, USA.

Alex Wang, Amanpreet Singh, Julian Michael, Felix Hill, Omer Levy, and Samuel R. Bowman. 2018. Glue: A multi-task benchmark and analysis platform for natural language understanding. *Learning*.

Peng Wang, An Yang, Rui Men, Junyang Lin, Shuai Bai, Zhikang Li, Jianxin Ma, Chang Zhou, Jingren Zhou, Hongxia Yang, and Chang Zhou¡ericzhou. 2022a. Unifying architectures, tasks, and modalities through a simple sequence-to-sequence learning framework.

Yue Wang, Shafiq Joty, Michael R. Lyu, Irwin King, Caiming Xiong, and Steven C. H. Hoi. 2020. Vd-bert: A unified vision and dialog transformer with bert. *arXiv: Computer Vision and Pattern Recognition*.

Yuxuan Wang, Xueliang Zhao, and Dongyan Zhao. 2022b. NLPCC-2022-Shared-Task-4.

Thomas Wolf, Lysandre Debut, Victor Sanh, Julien Chaumond, Clement Delangue, Anthony Moi, Pierric Cistac, Tim Rault, Rémi Louf, Morgan Funtowicz, Joe Davison, Sam Shleifer, Patrick von Platen, Clara Ma, Yacine Jernite, Julien Plu, Canwen Xu, Teven Le Scao, Sylvain Gugger, Mariama Drame, Quentin Lhoest, and Alexander M. Rush. 2020. Transformers: State-of-the-art natural language processing. In *Proceedings of the 2020 Conference on Empirical Methods in Natural Language Processing: System Demonstrations*, pages 38–45, Online. Association for Computational Linguistics.

Yuan Yao, Ao Zhang, Zhengyan Zhang, Zhiyuan Liu, Tat-Seng Chua, and Maosong Sun. 2022. Cpt: Colorful prompt tuning for pre-trained vision-language models.

Tong Ye, Shijing Si, Jianzong Wang, Rui Wang, Ning Cheng, and Jing Xiao. 2022. Vu-bert: A unified framework for visual dialog.

Hao Zhang, Aixin Sun, Wei Jing, and Joey Tianyi Zhou. 2020. Span-based localizing network for natural language video localization. *arXiv: Computation and Language*.

Songyang Zhang, Houwen Peng, Jianlong Fu, and Jiebo Luo. 2019a. Learning 2d temporal adjacent networks for moment localization with natural language. *national conference on artificial intelligence*.

Yizhe Zhang, Siqi Sun, Michel Galley, Yen-Chun Chen, Chris Brockett, Xiang Gao, Jianfeng Gao, Jingjing Liu, and Bill Dolan. 2019b. Dialogpt: Large-scale generative pre-training for conversational response generation. *meeting of the association for computational linguistics*.

Zhuosheng Zhang and Hai Zhao. 2021. Advances in multi-turn dialogue comprehension: A survey. *arXiv: Computation and Language*.

Hao Zhou, Pei Ke, Zheng Zhang, Yuxian Gu, Yinhe Zheng, Chujie Zheng, Yida Wang, Chen Henry Wu, Hao Sun, Xiaocong Yang, Bosi Wen, Xiaoyan Zhu, Minlie Huang, and Jie Tang. 2021. Eva: An open-domain chinese dialogue system with large-scale generative pre-training. *arXiv: Computation and Language*.

Model Transfer for Event Tracking as Transcript Understanding for Videos of Small Group Interaction

Sumit Agarwal, Rosanna Vitiello, Carolyn Penstein Rose
{sumita, rvitiell, cprose}@cs.cmu.edu
Language Technologies Institute, Carnegie Mellon University

Abstract

Videos of group interactions contain a wealth of information beyond the information directly communicated in a transcript of the discussion. Tracking who has participated throughout an extended interaction and what each of their trajectories has been in relation to one another is the foundation for joint activity understanding, though it comes with some unique challenges in videos of tightly coupled group work. Motivated by insights into the properties of such scenarios, including group composition and the properties of task-oriented, goal-directed tasks, we present a successful proof-of-concept. In particular, we present a transfer experiment to a dyadic robot construction task, an ablation study, and a qualitative analysis.

1 Introduction

The broad area of transcript understanding from video encompasses more than the information communicated through discussion, especially when the video captures small group interactions. In that case, each action is meaningful in the context of a broader task. From a social perspective, actions and reactions are meaningful in relation to one another. Sequences of actions of an individual within an interaction are meaningful as an enactment of role taking within a group activity. Building on recent work in multi-object tracking, which is a paradigm of interest in the computer vision community, this paper presents a proof-of-concept for model transfer for tracking the trajectories of participants within a small group activity. In particular, we target tightly coupled group work, which is challenging due to the close proximity of participants, intermittent motion, and periodic movement in and out of view. Success tracking within such scenarios is a key enabler for joint activity understanding, which requires at the foundation tracking who has participated throughout an extended interaction and what each of their trajectories has been in relation to one another. Our results demonstrate positive impact of three different enhancements motivated by consideration of the nature of tightly coupled collaborative group activities.

In many contexts of learning and work, dyads and small groups work together to accomplish a goal. The ability to understand a video capturing this type of interaction has many real world applications. For example, video recordings of such interactions are very common forms of data for research on group learning, communication, and group work. Real time understanding of group interactions has also been used to trigger support for group behavior in order to improve outcomes. Facilitators overseeing multiple groups can use reports of this real time understanding to support decision making regarding how they divide their attention between groups.

In the remainder of the paper, we first offer a review of related work both from the computer vision community and from the multi-modal learning analytics community. Next, we present our technical approach, extending recent successes using DeepSORT for Multiple Object Tracking (MOT). We then present a successful experiment producing results demonstrating improvement over a state-of-the-art baseline, as well as an ablation study to investigate the individual effects of each enhancement and a qualitative analysis of those effects.

2 Background & Related Work

From a technical perspective, the work reported in this paper has its roots in recent directions in the Multi-Object Tracking (MOT) literature. However, as the intended application is within areas of research and practice focused on supported group work and learning, we also review work from the field of Learning Analytics.

Proceedings of the 29th International Conference on Computational Linguistic, pages 20–29
October 12–17, 2022.

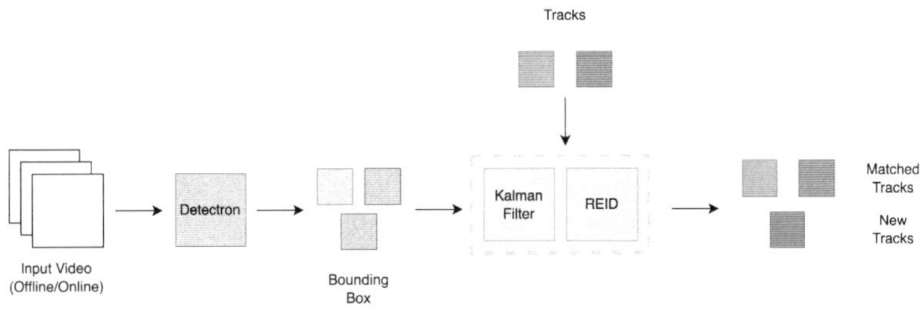

Figure 1: An overview of the DeepDSORT^{+} model architecture used in our experiments which extracts bounding boxes from frames using Detectron and then use Kalman Filter and REID based assignments to match previous tracks and create new unmatched tracks.

2.1 Multi-Object Tracking

In recent years, multi-object tracking has been a growing paradigm of interest in the computer vision community. The task requires the ability to detect multiple objects, mainly individual people, and consistently maintain their identities through the course of their trajectories given video input. The capability to successfully monitor trajectories grounds many high-level multimodal activities in video understanding, such as pose estimation and action recognition (Wang et al., 2013; Luo et al., 2017).

With advances in object detection and the popular MOT benchmark (Dendorfer et al., 2020), many state-of-the-art competitive tracking methods have emerged (Zhang et al., 2021; Wojke et al., 2017; Bewley et al., 2016). Offline models using batching strategies tend to perform well on the benchmark (Zhang et al., 2021). However, in domains where the goal is to achieve live video understanding, computationally efficient online tracking methods (Wojke et al., 2017; Bewley et al., 2016) that sequentially infer trajectories in real-time are preferred.

Despite advances in multi-object tracking, state-of-the-art models struggle with key issues, particularly in maintaining trajectory identities through occlusions and interactions among multiple objects. Our research in this paper shares the common goal of tackling these key issues directly, particularly in its exploration of group work in which complex interpersonal interactions are commonplace and are the necessary centerpiece to understanding dynamics of the activity.

2.2 Tracking Collaboration and Social Processes

In the field of Learning Sciences, automatic temporal analyzes of collaborative data have become essential to operationalize successful learning in student groups. Much of learning analytics has been focused around natural language data, particularly automated analysis of student discussion, which has consistently shown to be a valuable method in assessing student learning (Rosé et al., 2008; McLaren et al., 2007) and scaffolding engaging collaborative interactions (Kumar et al., 2007).

However, with the understanding that collaborative processes are innately multimodal, there is acknowledgment that traditional textual discourse may not tell the entire story. Consequently, multimodal learning analytics has become increasingly popular with the examination of visual patterns such as, in gesture, pose, and eye gaze. Recent studies have used multimodal data to detect misunderstandings during collaborative tasks (Cherubini et al., 2008), discover insights in learning processes (Spikol et al., 2018), and provide beneficial visual feedback to instructors in the classroom (Ahuja et al., 2019, 2021).

More broadly, collaborative learning analysis is one of many social processes that may benefit from precise multi-object tracking. In museums, visitor trajectories can provide curators with insights into improving interaction with content (Mezzini et al., 2020), and body tracking has been used to create immersive digital story telling exhibits (Genc and Häkkilä, 2021). Multi-object tracking is also applied in virtual reality (Uchiyama and Marchand, 2012), and provides information to create simulations for professional development, such as virtual reality for educators in the classroom (Ahuja et al., 2021). Our aim is to contribute to the ability to identify and maintain trajectories throughout videos, which provides an essential backbone and grounding for these detections in multimodal learning analytics.

3 Method

To perform tracking on videos in small group interaction, we explore the widely used online DeepSORT algorithm developed for Multiple-Object Tracking (MOT) benchmark. We extend the DeepSORT algorithm to improve transfer of the model from the task on which it was trained, namely tracking pedestrians walking on streets, to our group work setting. We begin with an explanation of the well-known DeepSORT algorithm and then discuss the extensions we have added.

3.1 DeepSORT

A tracking model must be able to detect bounding boxes, detect objects to track and continue to identify them for as long as they are in view, thus managing the lifespan of tracked objects. DeepSORT uses F-RCNN (Ren et al., 2015) or YOLO (Redmon and Farhadi, 2018), to detect bounding boxes on tracked objects. Building on SORT, DeepSORT also uses the Kalman filtering framework for track handling. Deviating from SORT, it uses CNN based appearance features for tracking as well, hence the prefix "Deep".

The algorithm considers two means for assigning tracks with bounding box detection, namely, one considering motion and the other considering appearance, captured in two different metrics, as shown in Figure 1.

Kalman Filter - Tracking is based on an 8-dimensional state space (u, v, r, h, $\hat{u}$, $\hat{v}$, $\hat{r}$, $\hat{h}$) that includes the center of the bounding box (u, v), the aspect ratio r and height h and their respective velocities in the image coordinates. A standard Kalman filter with constant velocity motion and linear observation models is used, where the bounding box (u, v, r, h) is considered a direct observation of the object state. It uses squared Mahalanobis distances between the predicted Kalman states and the newly arrived measurements.

$$d_m(i,j) = (d_j - y_i)^T S_i^{-1} (d_j - y_i)$$

where the i-th track distribution is projected into the measurement space as (y_i, S_i) and d_j, which is the j-th bounding box detection for the current frame. We use a high threshold of 0.95 for this distance in order to filter out unassociated detections.

REID - When the motion uncertainty across frames is high, the Mahalanobis distance is not a suitable metric. Also, during occlusions it is very difficult to apply Kalman filter based approaches for continuous frame tracking. Hence, appearance based features using person REID (reidentification) models becomes essential in those scenarios. For this, we compute appearance feature for each of the bounding boxes detected using a CNN-based REID and extract an appearance feature X^i for each track i, which is a function of the current appearance feature of the track x_i and previous X_i. We have used a simple CNN-based REID model to study the effectiveness of the algorithm in zero-shot transfer in our proof-of-concept experiment.

$$x_i = \text{REID}(\text{bounding\_box}(i))$$
$$X^i = f(x_i, X^i)$$

Next, the smallest cosine distance is applied between the previously computed F^i for the i-th track and the j-th detection feature r_j for the frame in consideration, in appearance space, with an admissible threshold, which we keep as 0.2.

$$d_a(i,j) = \min(1 - X^i r_j)$$

For the initial few frames, we use Kalman filter based assignment to confirm the initial set of tracks, and then after that we try matching with the appearance based features, because they are usually consistent across frames. For later frames, only when the appearance based features aren't able to match confirmed tracks with the bounding boxes or there are bounding boxes that are left undetected, we use Kalman Filter based assignment for matching. The metrics are complementary to each other, where the Kalman metric is usually used to recover from short-term motion-based assignments that are missed by appearance metrics, whereas the appearance metric helps to recover detection of objects having been lost from view from long-term occlusion.

3.2 Additions to DeepSORT

To the original DeepSORT algorithm, we introduce a set of enhancements to improve tracking in our target group work settings. We call the model with these changes DeepSORT$^+$. We explore a modification to DeepSORT to replace YOLO with

Detectron. We refer to the revised DeepSORT with Detectron as DeepDSORT, and the version with our enhancements DeepDSORT$^+$. Our proposed algorithm extensions are motivated from insights into tightly coupled group work, in particular, that the extended interaction involves a persistent set of participants who may move in and out of view but otherwise remain stable. Motion within view is related to the group work and thus purposeful. As such, it can be expected that changes in position across frames will be consistent over stretches of time. In summary, our enhancements include no longer deleting tracks with a maximum age, putting a limit on the number of tracks to be created, and introducing a smoothed version of the appearance feature. Our model with enhancements is shown in Figure 1.

3.2.1 No Max Age

DeepSORT uses a max age to maintain the life span of a track. It deletes tracks that have not been detected for a certain number of frames. Since DeepSORT was used for the MOT benchmark, which was used to track pedestrians from surveillance camera videos, it proved to be effective in that context where the total number of objects to track is unbounded, but if a track is not viewed for an extended time, they are unlikely to return. In our setting, the number of participants who are important to track is only the direct participants in the group work, and thus bounded. However, unlike pedestrians moving through an area, they may leave for an extended time, but will nevertheless likely return to the work. In this case, allowing for an unbounded number of tracks is superfluous, and as participants move in and out of view, their movement creates opportunities for false positive detection of new tracks. However, solving the problem by imposing a max age is counter-productive since the likelihood is high that tracks will return even if they have left for some time. Thus, we remove the max age constraint.

3.2.2 Number of tracks

Complementary to removing the max age constraint, we also take advantage of the bounded number of participants in the group work. There may be other people in view, in the background, moving through the space. Bounding the number of tracks reduces the propensity to lose track of a main participant and instead begin tracking someone in the background.

3.2.3 Smoothing appearance feature

In DeepSORT, current frame detections are compared with all previous frame features of tracks to find the closest track. Treating each frame separately introduces the possibility that two different tracks will appear similar. We mitigate this risk by using a smoothed global appearance feature F^i for each track i considering the current frame track feature f_i, given by the following formula.

$$F^i = \alpha * f_i + (1 - \alpha) * F^i$$

Reducing the set of observations of a track to a single smoothed version reduces the danger of a pair of frames from different tracks inadvertently appearing similar. For our experiments, we set α as 0.1, weighing heavily towards past observations and changing the representation only slowly over time.

3.2.4 Detectron

To identify bounding boxes, F-RCNN or YOLO based models have been shown to be very effective, which are also used in DeepSORT. Detectron (Wu et al., 2019) is an object detection model that is able to detect more concise human-based bounding boxes but with higher accuracy which is essential in our cases because the appearance features might confuse with the other people or objects if the bounding box is not very accurate in person position. We call this model DeepDSORT$^+$.

4 Experiments

4.1 Dataset

In order to evaluate our multimodal approach in small group activities and social processes, we collected and annotated an exploratory video corpus from a summer course conducted at Carnegie Mellon University. During the course, groups of 2-3 students participated in a robotic arm instruction task. The activity occurred over two collaborative sessions, each lasting around several hours: a robotic construction session in which students built their mechatronic arms and a robotic arm learning activity session in which students operated their robot. Each group collected video and audio data during each session using a Kodak Orbit 360 4K VR Camera with its 197° 4K Ultra Wide View Front Lens. Students were instructed to place each camera on a small tripod at the end of their table to capture every member of the group and the robotic arm.

	Dataset	MOTA ↑	MOTP ↑	IDF1 ↑	MT ↑	ML ↓	IDsw ↓	FP ↓	FN ↓
DeepSORT	Group 1	24.6	62.1	43.1	18.2	9.1	77	2229	2795
DeepSORT	Group 2	5.2	56.4	38.7	25	25	24	2274	2718
DeepSORT	Combined	15.4	59.7	41	21.6	17.1	101	4503	5513
DeepSORT$^+$	Group 1	31.2	62.8	52.7	18.2	18.2	22	1135	2613
DeepSORT$^+$	Group 2	6.3	56.5	46.1	25	25	16	1813	2463
DeepSORT$^+$	Combined	18.8	59.6	49.4	21.6	21.6	**19**	1474	2538
DeepDSORT$^+$	Group 1	78.1	89.9	85.9	63.6	9.1	36	165	1033
DeepDSORT$^+$	Group 2	93.1	90.3	96.5	100	0	20	92	204
DeepDSORT$^+$	Total	**85.6**	**90.1**	**91.2**	**81.8**	**4.6**	56	**257**	**1237**

Table 1: Combined results on our videos for DeepSORT, DeepSORT$^+$ and DeepDSORT$^+$ models. The arrow indicates whether higher value indicates a good (↑) or a bad (↓) result.

	MOTA ↑	MOTP ↑	IDF1 ↑	MT ↑	ML ↓	IDsw ↓	FP ↓	FN ↓
DeepDSORT$^+$	**85.6**	**90.1**	**91.2**	**81.8**	4.6	56	**257**	**1237**
DeepDSORT$^+$ − smooth	84.3	90.1	84.5	81.8	**0**	77	795	1824
DeepDSORT$^+$ − #tracks	83.6	90	85.6	77.3	0	78	957	1581
DeepDSORT$^+$ + max age	83.6	90.1	73.9	21.1	74.9	**15**	1842	2636

Table 2: Different ablations for our DeepDSORT$^+$ model on both groups of videos by removing each component that we introduce specifically for tracking group social processes.

These videos help study tracking in confined spaces with limited number of people in social processes. The videos feature many interactions between students and the robotic arm, as well as movement in different locations. Other complex scenarios include occasional off-camera movement, irrelevant background activity from other groups, and intermittent occlusions of students. Moreover, by using a video corpus collected via a small portable camera, social processes such as these may be collected and given support in real-time. Consequently, this corpus provides key scenarios that are essential to be able to track people consistently across frames for downstream automatic analysis of individual and group traits and outcomes.

We conduct our experiments across 2 student groups. We divided each video session into short 8 minute sections and extract about 500 frames with 1 fps for tracking annotation from every section. Each video has a gold standard tracking annotation created by extracting person class-based bounding boxes for each frame using F-RCNN and labeling each box with person IDs. In sum, we experimented with 4 8-minute videos from each group (8 videos in total), which comprises of 4148 annotated frames with a maximum of 3 students in a particular frame. People in the background of the frames uninvolved in the activity are not annotated because they are not part of the group collaboration.

4.2 Metrics

We evaluate our videos on metrics that have been commonly used for MOT benchmark, particularly we focus on the following values:

MOTA: Combines three error sources: false positives, missed targets and identity switches
MOTP: Misalignment between the predicted and ground-truth bounding boxes
IDF1: Ratio of correctly identified detections over the average of computed and ground-truth detections
MT: Mostly tracked targets that are tracked atleast 80% of their life span
ML: Mostly lost targets that are tracked atmost 20% of their life span
IDsw: Total no of identity switches
FP: Total no of false positives
FN: Total no of false negatives / missed targets

We highlight these metrics because they are crucial for further downstream applications concerning individual and group activity in social processes. That is, if models do not perform well on these metrics, they cannot perform an essential goal in multi-modal video understanding: identifying key roles and salient interactions during social processes. It is most important for models in this domain to accurately identify tracks and consistently maintain tracks without error. Additionally, we are most concerned with a model's ability to never lose or miss tracks in an activity, highlighting an emphasis on reducing false positives.

4.3 Experiments and Ablation

For both Group 1 and Group 2, we conduct the following experiments across variations of the DeepSORT model as described in 3:

- **DeepSORT** : original DeepSORT model as implemented by (Bewley et al., 2016) which uses YOLO to identify bounding boxes [1]
- **DeepSORT$^+$** : modified DeepSORT with YOLO and all additions mentioned in 3.2
- **DeepDSORT$^+$** : modified DeepSORT with Detectron [2] and all additions mentioned in 3.2

We also perform an ablation over the modified DeepDSORT$^+$ model through the removal of modified individual components:

- **DeepDSORT$^+$ − smooth** : modified Detectron DeepSORT without smoothing appearance feature
- **DeepDSORT$^+$ − # tracks** : modified Detectron DeepSORT without restriction of number of tracks
- **DeepDSORT$^+$ + max age** : modified Detectron DeepSORT with max age for tracking

For our experiments, we run the model over tracking for all the frames of the original video at 30 fps but the model is evaluated only on the gold-standard annotated frames extracted at 1 fps. We used 1 NVIDIA GTX 1080 GPU to run tracking over each video. Each frame takes a processing time of 0.18 s yielding a total of 5 fps. Running this online, in real time, would process 5 frames per second which is quite efficient for a tracking algorithm. This is another reason for choosing DeepSORT as the baseline because it is an ONLINE algorithm which is suitable for our purposes. For the CNN based Person REID model, we pretrain the model on the market1501 (Zheng et al., 2015) dataset, which is also used in the original DeepSORT implementation.

[1]https://github.com/mikel-brostrom/Yolov3_DeepSort_Pytorch

[2]https://github.com/facebookresearch/detectron2

5 Results

Table 1 shows the results of tracking over two sets of videos collected for two different groups, across DeepSORT, DeepSORT$^+$ and DeepDSORT$^+$ models. We can see that introducing the required components discussed in Section 3.2, to just the DeepSORT model, leads to a decrease in false positives and false negatives in DeepSORT$^+$. Further, we see improvements in almost all the metrics in DeepDSORT$^+$ showing that Detectron, in general, is a better model than YOLO, and our additional extensions lead to further improvement. Better bounding boxes implies better appearance features that make the appearance REID model less confused, leading to a drop in false positives and false negatives, thereby increasing IDF1. MOTA and MOTP metric also improve because the detected bounding boxes are closer to the ground-truth ones. We see that for Group2 videos the performance improvement is larger due to the Detectron model detecting people in the videos more accurately. There are more ID switches in the DeepDSORT$^+$ model than in DeepSORT$^+$, but significantly less than in DeepSORT. These ID switches account for a count of the frames in which the IDs are switched. The increased performance of DeepDSORT$^+$ implies that in the face of ID switches, it is able to recover.

6 Analysis

We perform ablation of our model to assess the impact of each of our extensions. Table 2 shows the results of removing each component. Figure 2 shows examples of qualitative errors introduced by removing each component compared to the complete model.

Smooth vs Non Smooth: For the smoothing ablation, instead of adding the new appearance feature as discussed in 3.2, we average all appearance features so that each frame feature receives equal importance such that smoothing is not applied. Without smoothing, abrupt changes in appearance or slight movement will likely change inference more drastically. We expect that without smoothing, the

(a) Tracking results when smoothing is not done and the features are averaged out for all the past frames, showing that it gives rise to false positives and ID switches. The upper results are DeepDSORT$^+$ results without smoothing and the lower ones are DeepDSORT$^+$ results.

(b) Tracking results when there is no cap on the number of tracks, showing that it gives rise to new tracks getting created when there is a slight mismatch in features (like when the person is in motion). The upper results are DeepDSORT$^+$ results without limit on number of tracks and the lower ones are DeepDSORT$^+$ results.

(c) Tracking results when maximum age is included as 100 frames, showing that when bounding box detections are missed in between frames or people move in and out of the frame, new IDs are created, (cyan to yellow). The upper results are DeepDSORT$^+$ results with maximum age and the lower ones are DeepDSORT$^+$ results.

Figure 2: Qualitative ablation results showing the removal of each component as discussed in Table 2, by removing smoothing in a), removing cap on number of tracks in b) and adding maximum age of tracks in c). Colors around bounding box indicate the track associated with the person, where a change in the color indicates an error made by the model.

model is more likely to confuse IDs when there is motion. Quantitatively, Table 2 supports this finding by revealing smoothing decreases ID switches and false positives.

In qualitative analysis of the smoothing ablation, we find errors that align with these expectations. Note in Figure 2a, the track in the purple bounding box is incorrectly switched when the individual leans forward in the non-smoothing model. However, with smoothing, the model correctly maintains their track. From this ablation, we conclude that smoothing helps decrease noise in abrupt changes of appearance in cases of obstruction and motion.

Limited vs Unlimited Number of Tracks: We also examine the ablation that removed the limit of the number of tracks that can be created. By limiting the maximum number of tracks to the number of participants within the activity, we hypothesized that the model would maintain tracks more consistently with less likelihood of creating irrelevant tracks during motion. The results in Table 2 support this hypothesis, as allowing the model to infer an unlimited number of tracks increased the rate of false positives.

This can be seen qualitatively in Figure 2b. Due to motion by the individual in the cyan bounding box, the ablation model mistakes motion for a new person and incorrectly creates a new yellow bounding box track around the individual. When tracks are limited, the model does not have the ability to create a new track and correctly maintains the identity of the moving individual.

No Max Age vs Max Age: In the maximum age ablation, we limit the maximum age of tracks to 100 frames. Originally, this threshold was used to remove unnecessary tracks that leave and never return in frame, commonly experienced in the benchmark MOT dataset. In collaborative social processes, the maximum age assumption was no longer appropriate. We noted that often individuals returned to the field of view after being occluded or out of frame for long periods of time, or they remain undetected by the model. By removing the max age threshold, we suspected the model would correctly maintain relevant tracks rather than discarding them.

This is quantitatively supported by the large increase in false positives and the decrease in IDF1 when a maximum age threshold of 100 frames was introduced. This can also be observed in Figure 2c, as the cyan bounding box individual is incorrectly discarded after leaving the frame and labeled as a new yellow bounding box individual when returning. This identity is correctly maintained without the maximum age threshold.

We note that keeping a higher maximum age threshold above 100 frames may also be a solution to this issue. However, it is impossible to define a generalizable amount of time for which people within a given activity will be out of frame. Hence, we conclude removing the maximum age threshold so that relevant tracks are never removed is the best approach for this modification.

7 Limitation

This paper targets tightly coupled group work, which is a closed setting with a fixed finite number of participants. If this assumption were required to be lifted, then people in the background might introduce the potential for false positives. A direction that would be valuable to explore in that case would be taking depth-perception into account in order to properly distinguish those engaged in the task from people in the background. As people move, their appearance changes, which introduces challenges for the matching process. One possible direction would be to tune the REID model over the first few frames when a new track appears. In order to further extend capabilities to participants who are easily confused, for example because of wearing similar clothing, more sophisticated REID models might be used that treat different body parts of individuals separately.

8 Conclusion

This paper presents a successful proof of concept for the transfer of models trained to track pedestrians to a scenario that features tightly coupled group work. With a small change to the original DeepSORT algorithm, using Detectron instead of YOLO, we are already able to achieve substantial improvement. Additional extensions motivated by the characteristics of tightly coupled group work add further improvement. In future work we play to explore more sophisticated REID models for this purpose. While this study lays the foundation for joint activity understanding, much is left to be done to explore aspects other than participant trajectories, such as the interplay of participant emotions and joint eye gaze.

Acknowledgements

This research was funded in part by NSF grants 2100401 and 1917955.

References

Karan Ahuja, Dohyun Kim, Franceska Xhakaj, Virag Varga, Anne Xie, Stanley Zhang, Jay Eric Townsend, Chris Harrison, Amy Ogan, and Yuvraj Agarwal. 2019. Edusense: Practical classroom sensing at scale. *Proc. ACM Interact. Mob. Wearable Ubiquitous Technol.*, 3(3).

Karan Ahuja, Deval Shah, Sujeath Pareddy, Franceska Xhakaj, Amy Ogan, Yuvraj Agarwal, and Chris Harrison. 2021. Classroom digital twins with instrumentation-free gaze tracking. CHI '21, New York, NY, USA. Association for Computing Machinery.

Alex Bewley, Zongyuan Ge, Lionel Ott, Fabio Ramos, and Ben Upcroft. 2016. Simple online and realtime tracking. In *2016 IEEE International Conference on Image Processing (ICIP)*, pages 3464–3468.

Mauro Cherubini, Marc-Antoine Nüssli, and Pierre Dillenbourg. 2008. Deixis and gaze in collaborative work at a distance (over a shared map): A computational model to detect misunderstandings. In *Proceedings of the 2008 Symposium on Eye Tracking Research Applications*, ETRA '08, page 173–180, New York, NY, USA. Association for Computing Machinery.

P. Dendorfer, H. Rezatofighi, A. Milan, J. Shi, D. Cremers, I. Reid, S. Roth, K. Schindler, and L. Leal-Taixé. 2020. Mot20: A benchmark for multi object tracking in crowded scenes. *arXiv:2003.09003[cs]*. ArXiv: 2003.09003.

Caglar Genc and Jonna Häkkilä. 2021. Using body tracking for involving museum visitors in digital storytelling. In *Augmented Humans Conference 2021*, AHs'21, page 304–306, New York, NY, USA. Association for Computing Machinery.

Rohit Kumar, Carolyn P. Rosé, Yi-Chia Wang, Mahesh Joshi, and Allen Robinson. 2007. Tutorial dialogue as adaptive collaborative learning support. In *Proceedings of the 2007 Conference on Artificial Intelligence in Education: Building Technology Rich Learning Contexts That Work*, page 383–390, NLD. IOS Press.

Chenxu Luo, Chang Ma, Chunyu Wang, and Yizhou Wang. 2017. Learning discriminative activated simplices for action recognition. *Proceedings of the AAAI Conference on Artificial Intelligence*, 31(1).

Bruce M. McLaren, Oliver Scheuer, Maarten De Laat, Rakheli Hever, Reuma De Groot, and Carolyn P. Rosé. 2007. Using machine learning techniques to analyze and support mediation of student e-discussions. In *Proceedings of the 2007 Conference on Artificial Intelligence in Education: Building Technology Rich Learning Contexts That Work*, page 331–338, NLD. IOS Press.

Mauro Mezzini, Carla Limongelli, Giuseppe Sansonetti, and Carlo De Medio. 2020. Tracking museum visitors through convolutional object detectors. In *Adjunct Publication of the 28th ACM Conference on User Modeling, Adaptation and Personalization*, UMAP '20 Adjunct, page 352–355, New York, NY, USA. Association for Computing Machinery.

Joseph Redmon and Ali Farhadi. 2018. Yolov3: An incremental improvement. *ArXiv*, abs/1804.02767.

Shaoqing Ren, Kaiming He, Ross Girshick, and Jian Sun. 2015. Faster r-cnn: Towards real-time object detection with region proposal networks. In *Advances in Neural Information Processing Systems*, volume 28. Curran Associates, Inc.

Carolyn Rosé, Yi-Chia Wang, Yue Cui, Jaime Arguello, Karsten Stegmann, Armin Weinberger, and Frank Fischer. 2008. Analyzing collaborative learning processes automatically: Exploiting the advances of computational linguistics in computer-supported collaborative learning. *I. J. Computer-Supported Collaborative Learning*, 3:237–271.

Daniel Spikol, Emanuele Ruffaldi, Giacomo Dabisias, and Mutlu Cukurova. 2018. Supervised machine learning in multimodal learning analytics for estimating success in project-based learning. *Journal of computer assisted learning.*, 34(4).

Hideaki Uchiyama and Eric Marchand. 2012. Object Detection and Pose Tracking for Augmented Reality: Recent Approaches. In *18th Korea-Japan Joint Workshop on Frontiers of Computer Vision (FCV)*, Kawasaki, Japan.

Chunyu Wang, Yizhou Wang, and Alan L. Yuille. 2013. An approach to pose-based action recognition. In *2013 IEEE Conference on Computer Vision and Pattern Recognition*, pages 915–922.

Nicolai Wojke, Alex Bewley, and Dietrich Paulus. 2017. Simple online and realtime tracking with a deep association metric. In *2017 IEEE International Conference on Image Processing (ICIP)*, pages 3645–3649. IEEE.

Yuxin Wu, Alexander Kirillov, Francisco Massa, Wan-Yen Lo, and Ross Girshick. 2019. Detectron2. `https://github.com/facebookresearch/detectron2`.

Yifu Zhang, Chunyu Wang, Xinggang Wang, Wenjun Zeng, and Wenyu Liu. 2021. Fairmot: On the fairness of detection and re-identification in multiple object tracking. *International Journal of Computer Vision*, 129:3069–3087.

Liang Zheng, Liyue Shen, Lu Tian, Shengjin Wang, Jingdong Wang, and Qi Tian. 2015. Scalable person re-identification: A benchmark. In *Computer Vision, IEEE International Conference on*.

BehanceMT: A Machine Translation Corpus for Livestreaming Video Transcripts

Minh Van Nguyen[1], **Franck Dernoncourt**[2], **and Thien Huu Nguyen**[1]
[1] Dept. of Computer and Information Science, University of Oregon, Eugene, OR, USA
[2] Adobe Research, Seattle, WA, USA
{minhnv,thien}@cs.uoregon.edu, dernonco@adobe.com

Abstract

Machine translation (MT) is an important task in natural language processing, which aims to translate a sentence in a source language to another sentence with the same/similar semantics in a target language. Despite the huge effort on building MT systems for different language pairs, most previous work focuses on formal-language settings, where text to be translated come from written sources such as books and news articles. As a result, such MT systems could fail to translate livestreaming video transcripts, where text is often shorter and might be grammatically incorrect. To overcome this issue, we introduce a novel MT corpus - BehanceMT for livestreaming video transcript translation. Our corpus contains parallel transcripts for 3 language pairs, where English is the source language and Spanish, Chinese, and Arabic are the target languages. Experimental results show that finetuning a pretrained MT model on BehanceMT significantly improves the performance of the model in translating video transcripts across 3 language pairs. In addition, the finetuned MT model outperforms GoogleTranslate in 2 out of 3 language pairs, further demonstrating the usefulness of our proposed dataset for video transcript translation. BehanceMT will be publicly released upon the acceptance of the paper.

1 Introduction

Machine Translation (MT) is an important and challenging task in natural language processing. Early work solved the task via statistical models (Al-Onaizan et al., 1999; Och et al., 2004; Lopez, 2008; Koehn, 2009). Recent work has made significant improvement via deep learning models (Luong et al., 2015; Vaswani et al., 2017; Devlin et al., 2019; Yang et al., 2019; Lewis et al., 2020) that formalize MT as a text generation task, where an encoder is used to consume input text in a source language and a decoder is employed to generate the input's translation in a target language. In addition to the advance in model design, another factor contributing to the success of deep learning models is the creation of enormous MT corpora for model training such as WMT corpora (Bojar et al., 2014, 2016), OPUS corpus (Tiedemann, 2012) and IWSLT corpus (Cettolo et al., 2015). However, these corpora often contain formal-language texts such as books and news articles. This could lead to poor performance of the MT models, which are pretrained on such corpora, on informal-language text such as video transcripts. This is unfortunate as video transcripts are being generated at growing rate in international online video platforms such as Youtube [1], Dailymotion [2], and Behance [3]. Video transcript translation is thus important to improve access to the platforms' content for users who speak different languages.

In this work, we aim to address this issue by introducing a novel MT corpus - BehanceMT for video transcript translation (VTT). BehanceMT contains transcripts collected from the Behance platform and translations obtained by human annotators for 3 language pairs, where English is the source language and Spanish, Chinese, and Arabic are the target languages. An MT system pretrained on formal-language corpora can then be finetuned on BehanceMT to improve its performance for VTT. To demonstrate this idea, we employ OpusMT (Tiedemann and Thottingal, 2020), which is a popular MT system pretrained on OPUS corpora. For each language pair, we finetune the pretrained OpusMT on the BehanceMT training data and evaluate the model (called OpusMT+) on the test data. Experimental results show that OpusMT+ consistently outperforms OpusMT in all settings across the three language pairs for VTT. In addition, we compare OpusMT+ with Google-

[1] https://www.youtube.com/
[2] https://www.dailymotion.com/
[3] https://www.behance.net/

Proceedings of the 29th International Conference on Computational Linguistic, pages 30–33
October 12–17, 2022.

Translate [4]. The significant improvement obtained by OpusMT+ over GoogleTranslate in English $\rightarrow$ Chinese and English $\rightarrow$ Spanish further demonstrates the usefulness of our proposed MT corpus. To facilitate future work for VTT, we will publicly release the BehanceMT corpus.

2 Related Work

Previous work has created different corpora for MT, such as WMT corpora (Bojar et al., 2014, 2016), OPUS corpus (Tiedemann, 2012) and IWSLT corpus (Cettolo et al., 2015). However, most of these corpora focus on formal-language settings. To the best of our knowledge, (Cettolo et al., 2015), which involves parallel TED talks, is the closest work to ours. However, TED talks are mostly presented in formal language. By contrast, BehanceMT is created based on transcripts of livestreaming videos, which are more informal.

3 Data

In this section, we present how we collect, preprocess, and annotate video transcripts to create the BehanceMT corpus.

3.1 Data Collection

Video transcripts in the BehanceMT corpus are collected from livestreaming videos on Behance, a platform for livestreaming tutorial videos on creative works such as digital drawing, graphic design, and photo/video editing. Each video transcript contains multiple sentences produced by the Microsoft Automatic Speech Recognition (ASR) system (Xiong et al., 2018). To achieve a diverse corpus given a fixed annotation budget, we randomly select 99 video transcripts and retain at most 50 first sentences with an average length of 10 words for each transcript. The resulting transcripts are finally used to perform data annotation.

3.2 Data Annotation

To translate the video transcripts, we hire crowd-sourcing workers on Upwork [5], who are native speakers of the target languages and proficient in English. Particularly, two crowd-sourcing workers are hired for translating video transcripts to Spanish, two crowd-sourcing workers are employed for translating video transcripts to Arabic, and one crowd-sourcing worker is hired for translating the video transcripts to Chinese. The workers are paid approximately $\$0.4$ for translating a sentence on average. Each worker performs the translation task by writing a translation for each sentence in an excel sheet containing their assigned video transcripts. To facilitate their annotation process, we also provide the video titles for each transcript so that the annotators can look up and watch the original videos if necessary.

Finally, we randomly split the translated video transcripts into train/dev/test parts with a ratio of $80/10/10$ for model development. The statistics for the resulting BehanceMT corpus is shown in Table 1.

Data	#transcripts	#sentences	#tokens
Train	78	3,787	40,024
Dev	11	530	5,007
Test	10	449	4,617

Table 1: Statistics for English data in BehanceMT corpus. Data for the target languages (Spanish, Arabic, and Chinese) contains the translations for each sentence in the English data.

4 Model

We employ OpusMT (Tiedemann and Thottingal, 2020) as the main model to conduct experiments on the proposed BehanceMT corpus. OpusMT uses the Marian-NMT architecture (Junczys-Dowmunt et al., 2018) and is pretrained on OPUS corpus (Tiedemann, 2012) to perform the translation task for different language pairs. For each of the three language pairs (i.e., English $\rightarrow$ Spanish, English $\rightarrow$ Arabic, English $\rightarrow$ Chinese), we further finetune the pretrained bilingual OpusMT model on the corresponding training data in BehanceMT. We denote the finetuned OpusMT model as OpusMT+.

5 Experiments

5.1 Model Training and Hyper-parameters

To implement the models, we use Pytorch 1.12.1 and Huggingface Transformers 4.21.1. The pretrained OpusMT models *"opus-mt-en-es"*, *"opus-mt-en-ar"*, and *"opus-mt-en-zh"* are obtained respectively for English $\rightarrow$ Spanish, English $\rightarrow$ Arabic, and English $\rightarrow$ Chinese settings from the official model hub [6]. To finetune the models on BehanceMT data, we employ Adam optimizer (Kingma and Ba, 2015) to train the model for 50

[4] https://translate.google.com/

[5] https://www.upwork.com/

[6] https://huggingface.co/Helsinki-NLP

epochs with a batch size of 16, a learning rate of $1e-6$, and a weight decay of 0.01.

Models	Spanish	Chinese	Arabic
OpusMT	35.0	5.3	25.2
OpusMT+	37.5	13.7	33.4
GoogleTranslate	34.9	3.1	43.2

Table 2: Model performance (BLEU score) comparison on BehanceMT test sets for the three target languages.

5.2 Performance Comparison

Table 2 presents performance comparison between OpusMT, OpusMT+, and GoogleTranslate across the three language pairs on test sets of our proposed BehanceMT corpus. First, we can see that OpusMT and GoogleTranslate perform poorly in most settings. This suggests that VTT is challenging task and more research effort is necessary to improve the performance for this area. Second, OpusMT+ significantly outperforms OpusMT in all settings, showing the benefit of finetuning OpusMT on video transcript data for improving model performance for VTT. This is further confirmed as OpusMT+ obtains significant improvement compared to the state-of-the-art commercial translation engine GoogleTranslate in two out of the three translation settings.

6 Conclusion

In this work, we present a novel corpus - BehanceMT for video transcript translation (VTT). Behance contains parallel video transcripts for three language pairs, where English is the source language and Spanish, Arabic, and Chinese are the target languages. Our experiments with strong baselines on BehanceMT show that the proposed corpus is challenging and useful for VTT across the three language pairs.

References

Yaser Al-Onaizan, Jan Curin, Michael Jahr, Kevin Knight, John Lafferty, Dan Melamed, Franz-Josef Och, David Purdy, Noah A Smith, and David Yarowsky. 1999. Statistical machine translation. In *Final Report, JHU Summer Workshop*, volume 30.

Ondrej Bojar, Christian Buck, Christian Federmann, Barry Haddow, Philipp Koehn, Johannes Leveling, Christof Monz, Pavel Pecina, Matt Post, Herve Saint-Amand, Radu Soricut, Lucia Specia, and Ales Tamchyna. 2014. Findings of the 2014 workshop on statistical machine translation. In *Proceedings of the Ninth Workshop on Statistical Machine Translation*, pages 12–58, Baltimore, Maryland, USA. Association for Computational Linguistics.

Ondrej Bojar, Rajen Chatterjee, Christian Federmann, Yvette Graham, Barry Haddow, Matthias Huck, Antonio Jimeno Yepes, Philipp Koehn, Varvara Logacheva, Christof Monz, Matteo Negri, Aurelie Neveol, Mariana Neves, Martin Popel, Matt Post, Raphael Rubino, Carolina Scarton, Lucia Specia, Marco Turchi, Karin Verspoor, and Marcos Zampieri. 2016. Findings of the 2016 conference on machine translation. In *Proceedings of the First Conference on Machine Translation*, pages 131–198, Berlin, Germany. Association for Computational Linguistics.

Mauro Cettolo, Jan Niehues, Sebastian Stüker, Luisa Bentivogli, Roldano Cattoni, and Marcello Federico. 2015. The IWSLT 2015 evaluation campaign. In *Proceedings of the 12th International Workshop on Spoken Language Translation: Evaluation Campaign*, pages 2–14, Da Nang, Vietnam.

Jacob Devlin, Ming-Wei Chang, Kenton Lee, and Kristina Toutanova. 2019. BERT: Pre-training of deep bidirectional transformers for language understanding. In *Proceedings of the 2019 Conference of the North American Chapter of the Association for Computational Linguistics: Human Language Technologies, Volume 1 (Long and Short Papers)*, pages 4171–4186, Minneapolis, Minnesota. Association for Computational Linguistics.

Marcin Junczys-Dowmunt, Roman Grundkiewicz, Tomasz Dwojak, Hieu Hoang, Kenneth Heafield, Tom Neckermann, Frank Seide, Ulrich Germann, Alham Fikri Aji, Nikolay Bogoychev, André F. T. Martins, and Alexandra Birch. 2018. Marian: Fast neural machine translation in C++. In *Proceedings of ACL 2018, System Demonstrations*, pages 116–121, Melbourne, Australia. Association for Computational Linguistics.

Diederik P. Kingma and Jimmy Ba. 2015. Adam: A method for stochastic optimization. In *3rd International Conference on Learning Representations, ICLR 2015, San Diego, CA, USA, May 7-9, 2015, Conference Track Proceedings*.

Philipp Koehn. 2009. *Statistical machine translation*. Cambridge University Press.

Mike Lewis, Yinhan Liu, Naman Goyal, Marjan Ghazvininejad, Abdelrahman Mohamed, Omer Levy, Veselin Stoyanov, and Luke Zettlemoyer. 2020. BART: Denoising sequence-to-sequence pre-training for natural language generation, translation, and comprehension. In *Proceedings of the 58th Annual Meeting of the Association for Computational Linguistics*, pages 7871–7880, Online. Association for Computational Linguistics.

Adam Lopez. 2008. Statistical machine translation. *ACM Computing Surveys (CSUR)*, 40(3):1–49.

Thang Luong, Hieu Pham, and Christopher D. Manning. 2015. Effective approaches to attention-based neural machine translation. In *Proceedings of the 2015 Conference on Empirical Methods in Natural Language Processing*, pages 1412–1421, Lisbon, Portugal. Association for Computational Linguistics.

Franz Josef Och, Daniel Gildea, Sanjeev Khudanpur, Anoop Sarkar, Kenji Yamada, Alexander Fraser, Shankar Kumar, Libin Shen, David A Smith, Katherine Eng, et al. 2004. A smorgasbord of features for statistical machine translation. In *Proceedings of the Human Language Technology Conference of the North American Chapter of the Association for Computational Linguistics: HLT-NAACL 2004*, pages 161–168.

Jörg Tiedemann. 2012. Parallel data, tools and interfaces in opus. In *Proceedings of the Eight International Conference on Language Resources and Evaluation (LREC'12)*, Istanbul, Turkey. European Language Resources Association (ELRA).

Jörg Tiedemann and Santhosh Thottingal. 2020. Opus-mt–building open translation services for the world. In *Proceedings of the 22nd Annual Conference of the European Association for Machine Translation*. European Association for Machine Translation.

Ashish Vaswani, Noam Shazeer, Niki Parmar, Jakob Uszkoreit, Llion Jones, Aidan N Gomez, Łukasz Kaiser, and Illia Polosukhin. 2017. Attention is all you need. *Advances in neural information processing systems*, 30.

Wayne Xiong, Lingfeng Wu, Fil Alleva, Jasha Droppo, Xuedong Huang, and Andreas Stolcke. 2018. The microsoft 2017 conversational speech recognition system. In *2018 IEEE international conference on acoustics, speech and signal processing (ICASSP)*, pages 5934–5938. IEEE.

Zhilin Yang, Zihang Dai, Yiming Yang, Jaime Carbonell, Russ R Salakhutdinov, and Quoc V Le. 2019. Xlnet: Generalized autoregressive pretraining for language understanding. *Advances in neural information processing systems*, 32.

Investigating the Impact of ASR Errors on Spoken Implicit Discourse Relation Recognition

Linh The Nguyen and **Dat Quoc Nguyen**
VinAI Research, Hanoi, Vietnam
{v.linhnt140, v.datnq9}@vinai.io

Abstract

We present an empirical study investigating the influence of automatic speech recognition (ASR) errors on the spoken implicit discourse relation recognition (IDRR) task. We construct a spoken dataset for this task based on the Penn Discourse Treebank 2.0 (Prasad et al., 2008). On this dataset, we conduct "Cascaded" experiments employing state-of-the-art ASR and text-based IDRR models and find that the ASR errors significantly decrease the IDRR performance. In addition, the "Cascaded" approach does remarkably better than an "End-to-End" one that directly predicts a relation label for each input argument speech pair.

original	Argument 1: computer-generated videos help
	Argument 2: the average american watches seven hours of tv a day
transcript	Argument 1: computer generated **vidio's health**
	Argument 2: the average american watches seven hours of **tevia** day

Table 1: An example of ASR errors (highlighted in bold). A prediction model needs to identify the discourse relation "Contingency.Cause.Reason" between Argument 1 and Argument 2, without the discourse marker (here, "since"), which is already challenging. It would be more challenging if the model is required to work on transcript data with potential ASR errors which might change the meanings of input arguments.

1 Introduction

Discourse parsing is one of the key research areas in NLP (Marcu, 2000; Li et al., 2022). One important problem in discourse parsing is the implicit discourse relation recognition (IDRR) task (Marcu and Echihabi, 2002), which aims to identify the relation between two discourse arguments (e.g. clauses, sentences or paragraphs in the document) without explicit discourse connectives (e.g., *but*, *and*, *because* and the like). This IDRR task has attracted many research works (Lin et al., 2009; Zhou et al., 2010; Ji and Eisenstein, 2015; Bai and Zhao, 2018; Nguyen et al., 2019; Kim et al., 2020; Dou et al., 2021; Jiang et al., 2021), and it is very useful for many downstream NLP tasks such as machine translation (Joty et al., 2017; Guzmán et al., 2014), text summarization (Li and Rafi, 2019; Gerani et al., 2014) and question answering (Chai and Jin, 2004; Jansen et al., 2014).

Implicit discourse relations also play essential roles in spoken language understanding tasks (Aubin et al., 2019; Ma et al., 2019). Thus, it is worth investigating the IDRR task in spoken form. Research works have been performed for IDRR from the manual speech transcripts (Pettibone and Pon-Barry, 2003; Tonelli et al., 2010; Rehbein et al., 2016). However, to the best of our knowledge, no study has investigated the effect of automatic speech recognition (ASR) errors on the spoken IDRR task. Table 1 shows an example of ASR errors that might affect the IDRR result.

In this paper, we present a study that investigates the influence of ASR errors on the downstream spoken IDRR task. As there is no public benchmark dataset for this spoken IDRR task, we construct a dataset for this task based on the Penn Discourse Treebank (PDTB) 2.0 (Prasad et al., 2008). Following previous works (Lee et al., 2018; You et al., 2020; Song et al., 2022) that construct spoken derivatives of text-based question answering and text-to-SQL datasets, we use the Google text-to-speech system to produce a spoken variant of the PDTB 2.0 dataset. In our "Cascaded" experiments combining state-of-the-art ASR and text-based IDRR models, we find that the ASR errors significantly decrease the performance of the downstream IDRR task. We also experiment with an "End-to-End" approach that directly predicts a relation label for each input argument speech pair, and find that the "End-to-End" obtains remarkably lower performances than the "Cascaded".

Proceedings of the 29th International Conference on Computational Linguistic, pages 34–39
October 12–17, 2022.

Statistic	#Pair	#Hour	WER
Training	12632	58.37	28.42
Validation	1183	5.42	27.28
Test	1046	4.59	30.27

Table 2: Our dataset statistics. "#Pair", "#Hour" and "WER" denote the number of spoken pairs, the number of speech audio hours and the word error rate, respectively. Here the word error rate is computed for the automatic transcripts predicted by Wav2Vec 2.0 w.r.t. the original text arguments.

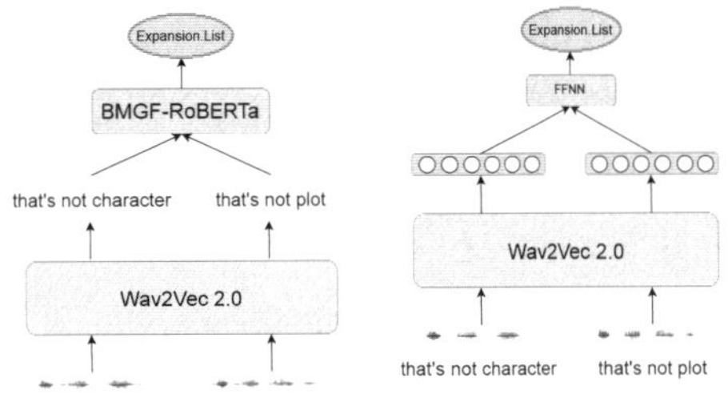

Figure 1: Illustrations of our empirical approaches: "Cascaded" in the left-hand side subfigure and "End-to-End" in the right-hand side subfigure.

2 Dataset construction

This section presents the dataset construction process for our spoken IDRR task. We construct our dataset in the spoken form based on the PDTB 2.0 dataset (Prasad et al., 2008), which is one of the largest benchmark datasets used for IDRR research. We employ the Google text-to-speech system to generate spoken variants of the original text arguments from the PDTB 2.0 dataset. We thus obtain speech pairs and the gold relation label for each speech pair (i.e. the label of the original argument pair). We also employ the standard PDTB 2.0 data split (Ji and Eisenstein, 2015) that uses sections 2–20, 0–1 and 21–22 for training, validation and test, respectively. Table 2 shows the statistics of our dataset.

3 Empirical approach

On our spoken dataset, we compare two implicit discourse relation recognition approaches: *Cascaded* vs. *End-to-End*.

3.1 Cascaded

The "Cascaded" approach combines two main components of automatic speech recognition (ASR) and text-based IDRR, as illustrated in Figure 1.

For the ASR component, we employ the base version of Wav2Vec 2.0 (Baevski et al., 2020)—which is pre-trained and fine-tuned on the 960-hour Librispeech dataset (Panayotov et al., 2015). In particular, we feed the spoken argument audios into Wav2Vec 2.0 to generate the corresponding automatic speech recognition (ASR) transcripts. For each argument speech pair, we thus obtain a corresponding transcript pair generated by Wav2Vec 2.0. Table 1 shows an example of ASR transcription errors from our training set. Table 2 also presents the word error rate of Wav2Vec 2.0 on our dataset.

The text-based IDRR component takes each speech transcript pair produced by the ASR component as input and predicts the discourse relation label for the transcript pair. For IDRR, we employ BMGF-RoBERTa (Liu et al., 2020) with its officially public implementation, which still maintains its state-of-the-art performance level up to date on the PDTB 2.0 dataset. BMGF-RoBERTa employs RoBERTa (Liu et al., 2019) to obtain contextualized representations for word tokens in each argument and also uses the following modules:

- Trainable segment embeddings (**SE**): the trainable segment embeddings are originally used in BERT (Devlin et al., 2019), but removed in RoBERTa. BMGF-RoBERTa employs these embeddings because they are shown to be helpful for the IDRR task (Shi and Demberg, 2019).
- Bilateral Matching (**BM**): comparing each word token of one argument against all tokens of the other one and vice versa.
- Gated Fusion (**GF**): assigning different importance to each word token in arguments, and then aggregating importance results and encoding each argument into a vector representation.
- Prediction: Two arguments' vectors are concatenated into a single one that is fed into a two-layer feed-forward neural network (FFNN) followed by a `softmax` for relation classification.

3.2 End-to-End

For the "End-to-End" approach, we propose a speech-based discourse identification model that takes each argument speech pair as input and directly predicts the relation label for the input speech pair. In particular, the model employs Wav2Vec 2.0 to extract a feature vector representation from each speech. The model uses a similar prediction layer as in BMGF-RoBERTa, which concatenates two audios' vectors into a single vector and then feeds this vector into a two-layer FFNN followed by a `softmax` for relation classification. Figure 1 also illustrates the "End-to-End" architecture.

3.3 Implementation details and Setup

For the "Cascaded" approach, we train BMGF-RoBERTa for 40 epochs on the speech transcript pairs from the training set. We employ optimal hyper-parameters from Liu et al. (2020), which are 0.001, 32 and 0.005 for the Adam learning rate, the batch size and the weight decay, respectively. In each training epoch, we compute the model's accuracy two times on the validation set of speech transcript pairs to select the best checkpoint. The selected checkpoint is then applied to the test set of speech transcript pairs to report final results.

For the "End-to-End", Wav2Vec 2.0 is employed as a feature extractor, frozen during training, while the remaining prediction layer is learned. We train the proposed model for 10 epochs on the speech pairs from the training set, using the Adam learning rate grid-searched at 1e-5 with a batch size of 1 (as the audios are long) and 8 gradient accumulation steps. We evaluate the model two times on the validation set of speech pairs in each training epoch, to select the best checkpoint to apply to the test set.

Note that PDTB 2.0 has a hierarchical annotation scheme of 3 implicit relation levels. Most works using PDTB 2.0 report *accuracy* (Acc.) and *macro-averaged F1* scores for the classification of all **4** labels from the top level (**L1**), including Comparison (*Comp.*), Contingency (*Cont.*), Expansion (*Exp.*) and Temporal (*Temp.*). Recent works (Ji and Eisenstein, 2015; Bai and Zhao, 2018; Dai and Huang, 2019; Shi and Demberg, 2019; Liu et al., 2020) additionally report *accuracy* (Acc.) scores for the classification of the top **11** frequent labels from the second level (**L2**). We follow the recent works to report obtained results on both setups.

4 Experimental results

4.1 Main results

Table 3 reports multi-class classification results obtained on the test set at the top (L1) and second (L2) levels. When it comes to the effect of ASR errors propagation, all performance scores are significantly decreased: 69.06% → 66.63% and 58.13% → 50.24%, which are classification accuracies for the top- and second-level labels, respectively; and

Model	4-way L1 (Acc. | F1)	11-way L2 (Acc.)
Liu et al.	69.06 | 63.39	58.13
Cascaded	66.63 | 56.00	50.24
End-to-End	51.34 | 38.29	37.92

Table 3: Multi-class classification results (in %) on the test set. "Liu et al." denotes results of BMGF-RoBERTa with the original text arguments as its input (i.e. equivalent to a perfect ASR of 0% WER). Each score difference between two models is significant with p-value < 0.01.

Model	Exp.	Comp.	Cont.	Temp.
Liu et al.	77.66	59.44	60.98	50.26
Cascaded	74.15	56.78	57.28	43.64
End-to-End	58.15	38.39	37.64	28.32

Table 4: Binary classification F1 score (in %) for each L1 label on the test set. Each score difference between two models is significant with p-value < 0.01.

63.39% → 56.00%, which are F_1 scores for the top-level label prediction. Table 4 shows the one-vs-rest binary classification F1 score for each label from the top level. ASR errors also remarkably reduce the performance. In particular, scores are decreased about 3% on the Expansion (77.66% → 74.15%), Comparison (59.44% → 56.78%) and Contingency (60.98% → 57.28%) labels, and about 7% on the Temporal label (50.26% → 43.64%).

Tables 3 and 4 also show that the performance of the "End-to-End" approach is far behind the "Cascaded" one's. For example, the accuracy and F1 scores obtained for "End-to-End" on the top-level labels are about 15+% lower than those of "Cascaded". This is not surprising because: (1) our speech dataset is small for this difficult language understanding task of spoken IDRR, and (2) the "Cascaded" approach gets to utilize the powerful pre-trained RoBERTa model while the "End-to-End" one is limited to a simple two-layer FFNN.

4.2 Ablation study

We conduct an ablation study to investigate the contribution of each main module of the BMGF-RoBERTa model to the final results of the "Cascaded" approach. Table 5 shows the results obtained on the validation set. Each of the main modules, including the trainable segment embeddings, the Bilateral Matching and Gated Fusion, plays an essential role in BMGF-RoBERTa (See Section 3.1 for brief descriptions of these modules). Removing

Model	4-way L1 (Acc. | F1)	11-way L2 (Acc.)	Exp.	Comp.	Cont.	Temp.
Cascaded	**68.13 | 58.16**	**54.59**	**77.63**	**58.33**	**57.23**	**40.26**
(1) w/o SE	62.64 | 49.09	47.04	75.07	43.69	54.02	35.68
(2) w/o BM	66.27 | 57.66	51.59	76.46	52.80	54.96	38.98
(3) w/o GF	66.53 | 55.95	51.93	75.98	55.24	55.76	33.66
(1) & (2) & (3)	59.59 | 49.02	43.00	73.77	43.41	47.91	29.91

Table 5: Ablation results on the validation set. **(1)** w/o SE: Without employing the trainable segment embeddings; **(2)** w/o BM: Without the Bilateral Matching module; **(3)** w/o GF: Without the Gated Fusion module. Each score difference between the full cascaded model and its ablated one is significant with p-value < 0.01.

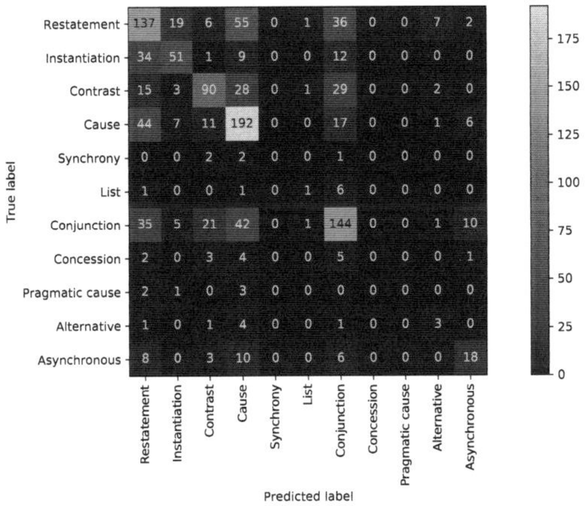

Figure 2: The confusion matrix of the "Cascaded" approach on the validation set w.r.t. the top 11 frequent labels from the second level.

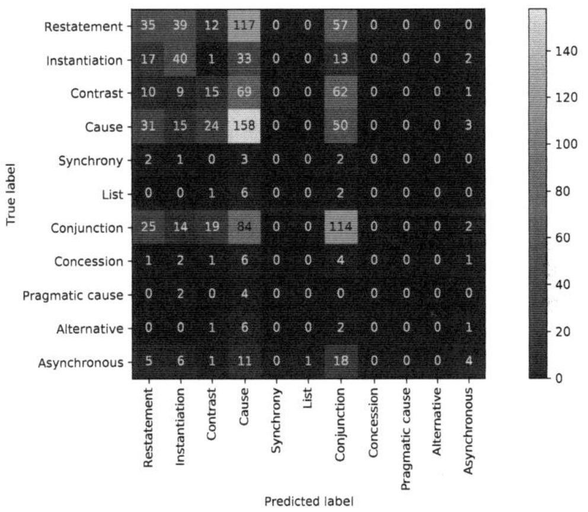

Figure 3: The confusion matrix of the "End-to-End" approach on the validation set w.r.t. the top 11 frequent labels from the second level.

each module significantly reduces the performance. In addition, removing all three modules degrades the obtained results by about 10+% in most cases.

4.3 Error analysis

Figure 2 presents the confusion matrix of the "Cascaded" approach on the validation set w.r.t. multi-class classification of the top 11 frequent labels from the second level. We find that correct predictions mainly come from 6 major labels of *Cause*, *Conjunction*, *Restatement*, *Contrast*, *Instantiation* and *Asynchronous*. We also find that main errors come from the confusion between the relations *Restatement* and *Cause*, the relations *Conjunction* and *Cause* and the relations *Contrast* and *Conjunction*. They are difficult to distinguish because the form of the discourse unit in the two relation labels is semantically similar. We observe similar findings for the "End-to-End" as shown in Figure 3.

We provide a qualitative example to demonstrate the challenges of this spoken IDRR task. Given an input speech pair of the original text argument pair ("*After the race, Fortune 500 executives* ***drooled*** *like schoolboys over the cars and drivers*", "*No dummies, the drivers pointed out they still had space on their machines for another sponsor's name or two*"), in the "Cascaded" approach, the original token "**drooled**" from the first argument is incorrectly predicted as **druled** by the ASR component. Both the "Cascaded" and "End-to-End" approaches produce an incorrect label prediction of *Contrast*, while BMGF-RoBERTa takes this original text argument pair as input and produces a correct label of *Cause*.

5 Discussion

The method of employing the Google text-to-speech to generate spoken forms of the original text arguments in the PDTB 2.0 dataset produces an artificially generated dataset, thus not fully reflecting the error types of human speech. In addition, the original raw PDTB 2.0 dataset comes from the Wall Street Journal (WSJ) articles. So our dataset might not cover relevant real-world spoken genres.

We unfortunately were unaware of the availability of the Continuous Speech Recognition (CSR) corpus that consists of human-read speech with texts from the WSJ when conducting our study.[1] There might be an overlap between original texts from the PDTB 2.0 dataset and the CSR corpus, thus the overlap might be used for further evaluation in future work.

6 Conclusion

We have presented an empirical study investigating the influence of ASR errors on the spoken IDRR task. We construct a spoken derivative of the PDTB 2.0 dataset and conduct "Cascaded" experiments employing state-of-the-art ASR and text-based IDRR models on this spoken dataset. We find that the ASR errors significantly reduce the IDRR performance. We also find that an "End-to-End" approach that directly predicts a relation label for each input speech pair obtains remarkably lower performances than the "Cascaded" one.

References

Adèle Aubin, Alessandra Cervone, Oliver Watts, and Simon King. 2019. Improving Speech Synthesis with Discourse Relations. In *Proceedings of INTERSPEECH*, pages 4470–4474.

Alexei Baevski, Yuhao Zhou, Abdelrahman Mohamed, and Michael Auli. 2020. wav2vec 2.0: A framework for self-supervised learning of speech representations. In *Proceedings of NeurIPS*, pages 12449–12460.

Hongxiao Bai and Hai Zhao. 2018. Deep Enhanced Representation for Implicit Discourse Relation Recognition. In *Proceedings of COLING*, pages 571–583.

Joyce Y. Chai and Rong Jin. 2004. Discourse Structure for Context Question Answering. In *Proceedings of the Workshop on Pragmatics of Question Answering at HLT-NAACL 2004*, pages 23–30.

Zeyu Dai and Ruihong Huang. 2019. A Regularization Approach for Incorporating Event Knowledge and Coreference Relations into Neural Discourse Parsing. In *Proceedings of EMNLP-IJCNLP*, pages 2976–2987.

Jacob Devlin, Ming-Wei Chang, Kenton Lee, and Kristina Toutanova. 2019. BERT: Pre-training of Deep Bidirectional Transformers for Language Understanding. In *Proceedings of NAACL*, pages 4171–4186.

[1] https://catalog.ldc.upenn.edu/LDC94S13A

Zujun Dou, Yu Hong, Yu Sun, and Guodong Zhou. 2021. CVAE-based Re-anchoring for Implicit Discourse Relation Classification. In *Findings of EMNLP*, pages 1275–1283.

Shima Gerani, Yashar Mehdad, Giuseppe Carenini, Raymond T. Ng, and Bita Nejat. 2014. Abstractive Summarization of Product Reviews Using Discourse Structure. In *Proceedings of EMNLP*, pages 1602–1613.

Francisco Guzmán, Shafiq Joty, Lluís Màrquez, and Preslav Nakov. 2014. Using Discourse Structure Improves Machine Translation Evaluation. In *Proceedings of ACL*, pages 687–698.

Peter Jansen, Mihai Surdeanu, and Peter Clark. 2014. Discourse Complements Lexical Semantics for Non-factoid Answer Reranking. In *Proceedings of ACL*, pages 977–986.

Yangfeng Ji and Jacob Eisenstein. 2015. One Vector is Not Enough: Entity-Augmented Distributed Semantics for Discourse Relations. *Transactions of the ACL*, 3:329–344.

Feng Jiang, Yaxin Fan, Xiaomin Chu, Peifeng Li, and Qiaoming Zhu. 2021. Not Just Classification: Recognizing Implicit Discourse Relation on Joint Modeling of Classification and Generation. In *Proceedings of EMNLP*, pages 2418–2431.

Shafiq Joty, Francisco Guzmán, Lluís Màrquez, and Preslav Nakov. 2017. Discourse Structure in Machine Translation Evaluation. *Computational Linguistics*, 43:683–722.

Najoung Kim, Song Feng, Chulaka Gunasekara, and Luis Lastras. 2020. Implicit Discourse Relation Classification: We Need to Talk about Evaluation. In *Proceedings of ACL*, pages 5404–5414.

Chia-Hsuan Lee, Szu-Lin Wu, Chi-Liang Liu, and Hung yi Lee. 2018. Spoken SQuAD: A Study of Mitigating the Impact of Speech Recognition Errors on Listening Comprehension. In *Proceedings of INTERSPEECH*, pages 3459–3463.

J. Li and M. Rafi. 2019. Utilize Discourse Relations to Segment Document for Effective Summarization. In *Proceedings of SKG*, pages 12–15.

Jiaqi Li, Ming Liu, Bing Qin, and Ting Liu. 2022. A survey of discourse parsing. *Frontiers of Computer Science*, 16(5).

Ziheng Lin, Min-Yen Kan, and Hwee Tou Ng. 2009. Recognizing Implicit Discourse Relations in the Penn Discourse Treebank. In *Proceedings of EMNLP*, pages 343–351.

Xin Liu, Jiefu Ou, Yangqiu Song, and Xin Jiang. 2020. On the Importance of Word and Sentence Representation Learning in Implicit Discourse Relation Classification. In *Proceedings of IJCAI*, pages 3830–3836.

Yinhan Liu, Myle Ott, Naman Goyal, Jingfei Du, Mandar Joshi, Danqi Chen, Omer Levy, Mike Lewis, Luke Zettlemoyer, and Veselin Stoyanov. 2019. RoBERTa: A Robustly Optimized BERT Pretraining Approach. *arXiv preprint*, arXiv:1907.11692.

Mingyu Derek Ma, Kevin Bowden, Jiaqi Wu, Wen Cui, and Marilyn Walker. 2019. Implicit Discourse Relation Identification for Open-domain Dialogues. In *Proceedings of ACL*, pages 666–672.

Daniel Marcu. 2000. *The Theory and Practice of Discourse Parsing and Summarization*. MIT Press.

Daniel Marcu and Abdessamad Echihabi. 2002. An Unsupervised Approach to Recognizing Discourse Relations. In *Proceedings of ACL*, pages 368–375.

Linh The Nguyen, Linh Van Ngo, Khoat Than, and Thien Huu Nguyen. 2019. Employing the Correspondence of Relations and Connectives to Identify Implicit Discourse Relations via Label Embeddings. In *Proceedings of ACL*, pages 4201–4207.

Vassil Panayotov, Guoguo Chen, Daniel Povey, and Sanjeev Khudanpur. 2015. Librispeech: An ASR corpus based on public domain audio books. In *Proceedings of ICASSP*, pages 5206–5210.

Jeanette Pettibone and Heather Pon-Barry. 2003. A Maximum Entropy Approach to Recognizing Discourse Relations in Spoken Language. Technical report, Stanford University.

Rashmi Prasad, Nikhil Dinesh, Alan Lee, Eleni Miltsakaki, Livio Robaldo, Aravind Joshi, and Bonnie Webber. 2008. The Penn Discourse TreeBank 2.0. In *Proceedings of LREC*.

Ines Rehbein, Merel Scholman, and Vera Demberg. 2016. Annotating Discourse Relations in Spoken Language: A Comparison of the PDTB and CCR Frameworks. In *Proceedings of LREC*, pages 1039–1046.

Wei Shi and Vera Demberg. 2019. Next Sentence Prediction helps Implicit Discourse Relation Classification within and across Domains. In *Proceedings of EMNLP-IJCNLP*, pages 5790–5796.

Yuanfeng Song, Raymond Chi-Wing Wong, Xuefang Zhao, and Di Jiang. 2022. Speech-to-SQL: Towards Speech-driven SQL Query Generation From Natural Language Question. *ArXiv preprint*, arxiv:2201.01209.

Sara Tonelli, Giuseppe Riccardi, Rashmi Prasad, and Aravind Joshi. 2010. Annotation of Discourse Relations for Conversational Spoken Dialogs. In *Proceedings of LREC*.

Chenyu You, Nuo Chen, Fenglin Liu, Dongchao Yang, and Yuexian Zou. 2020. Towards Data Distillation for End-to-end Spoken Conversational Question Answering. *ArXiv preprint*, arxiv:2010.08923.

Zhi-Min Zhou, Yu Xu, Zheng-Yu Niu, Man Lan, Jian Su, and Chew Lim Tan. 2010. Predicting Discourse Connectives for Implicit Discourse Relation Recognition. In *Proceedings of COLING: Posters*, pages 1507–1514.

Author Index